SECURITY ENHANCEMENT OF BIG DATA ANALYSIS USING ARTIFICIAL INTELLIGENCE

SEBDA-AI

DR. VIRENDRA KUMAR SWARNKAR

Contents

Contents

Preface

In this book, Protecting the privacy of computer networks containing consumer data is a vital concern for people, businesses, and governments. There has been a spike in threats/attacks on famous websites as attacks against networked networks are becoming more frightening and new techniques to target them are being used every day. Additionally, intrusion protection is used to prevent outside attempts by hackers and scammers. One approach to developing an intrusion detection system (IDS) is by learning from human-written traffic logs. Currently, the IDS needs two essential, discriminating and representative characteristics, all in order to have a high accuracy. An example is the "sparse" or "dimensionality" reduction strategies AE and PCA (PCA). The attribute extraction strategies employed by the speech recognition market are then used to create an RF classification simulation technique with K-Mean Cluster. The attempt to reduce the features of the dataset "CICIDs" from 78 to 45 is going to reduce the features of the dataset from 78 to 45 while maintaining a high precision of 99.7% in the Random Forest classifier with k-means clustering.Protecting the privacy of computer networks containing consumer data is a vital concern for people, businesses, and governments. There has been a spike in threats/attacks on famous websites as attacks against networked networks are becoming more frightening and new techniques to target them are being used every day. Additionally, intrusion protection is used to prevent outside attempts by hackers and scammers. One approach to developing an intrusion detection system (IDS) is by learning from human-written traffic logs. Currently, the IDS needs two essential, discriminating and representative characteristics, all in order to have a high accuracy. An example is the "sparse" or "dimensionality" reduction strategies AE and PCA (PCA). The attribute extraction strategies employed by the speech recognition market are then used to create an RF classification simulation technique with K-Mean Cluster. The attempt to reduce the features of the dataset "CICIDs" from 78 to 45 is going to reduce the features of the dataset from 78 to 45 while maintaining a high precision of 99.7% in the Random Forest classifier with k-means clustering.

Dr. Virendra Kumar Swarnkar
Dr. Suman Kumar Swarnkar

Acknowledgements

I would like to express my sincere appreciation to **Dr. Suman Kumar Swarnkar,** Assistant Professor, Shri Shankaracharya Institute of Professional Management and Technology, Raipur and **Dr. Asha Ambhaikar,** Professor & Dean Students Welfare, Kalinga University, New Raipur, who has been constant in her valuable guidance and encouragement in my this book. During my book they has offered guidance, and also for generating newer ideas. Above all and the most needed, they provided me unflinching encouragement and support in various ways.

I want to thank my parents, **Mr. Ravindra Kumar Swarnkar** and **Mrs. Lata Swarnkar** who raised me with the hearts and provided me the best education in those hard days.

I would like to specially thank my wife **Smt. Bharti Swarnkar** for patiently waiting for me and also for providing constant support for completion of this work.

Finally, I would like to thank everybody who was important to the successful realization of thesis, as well as expressing my apology that I could not mention personally one by one.

Dr. Virendra Kumar Swarnkar
Dr. Suman Kumar Swarnkar

CHAPTER ONE

Introduction

1.1 Big Data Security

1.1 Big Data Security

Big data analytics are being adopted in each field today and are increasing exponentially. If you prepare for big data beforehand, so there are great ways to activate your company successfully. The task is, however, to include a large number of brands, collaborators, clients and other data to the Big Data Analytics systems. In general, this data may not have adequate data protection and provides cyber attackers with a great opportunity. Big data protection and confidentiality sensitivities remain a challenge to resolve. Smart analysis has been developed with the help of the proposed security intelligence model to improve the safety. The method and measurements used to protect both data and analytical processes may be called Big Data protection. Big data security mostly aims to defend against hacks, robberies and other harmful activities which could damage sensitive information. For the organizations working in the cloud, big data protection issues are multi-faceted. This daunting challenge involves identity manipulation that can crash a computer online, malware or DDoS. [1]

From a security perspective, the toughest problem is protecting the privacy of users. Big data also includes enormous volumes of sensitive knowledge, and is of major concern to users' privacy. Infringements surrounding big data may have more devastating effects than we usually see in the news, as a result of the volume of data stored. That is because a huge number of individuals with credibility and immense judicial implications may suffer from a breakdown in the protection of Big Data. Organizations must maintain a proper compromise between the usefulness of the information and privacy when generating Big Data Information. It should be properly anonymized until the details were saved and every special identity for a person should be removed. It can be a protection problem, as it may not be sufficient to delete unique identifiers and ensure that the data remains confidential.[2]

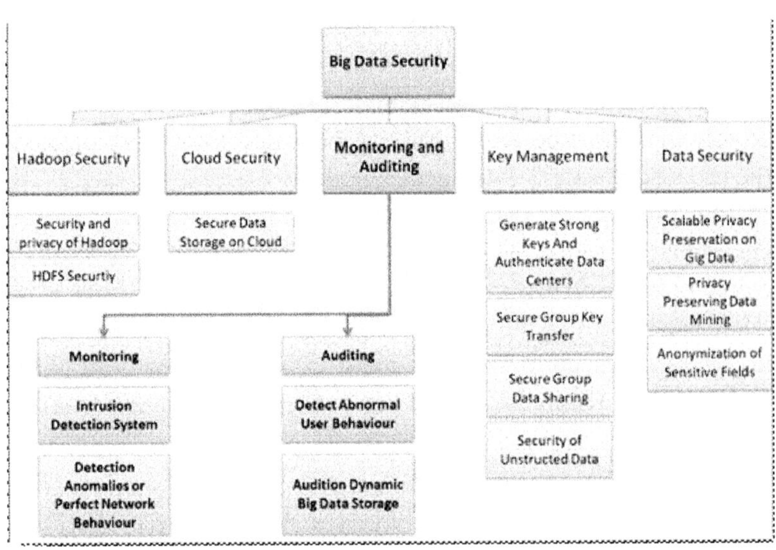

Figure 1.1 Areas of big data protection

1.2 Big Data Security Technologies

1.2 Big Data Security Technologies

No new techniques are available for big data protection. Their scalability and their ability to protect many data forms in various stages are recent.

- **Intrusion protection system:** safety workhorses are intruders detection and avoidance programs. This makes the big data network no less useful. The importance of large data and the distributed model are suitable for attempts at interference. IPS allows security administrators to defend the Big Data infrastructure from attack, and IDS can quarantine the intrusion until significant harm is done if intrusion succeeds.
- **Encryption:** The data must be secured in the transit and residual way by the encryption software and done by large quantities of data. Encryption must also work on various forms of data provided by the user and the computer. The encryption tools will have to deal with various analytical tools, their outcomes and standard big data storage formats like RDBMS, non-relation databases such as NoSQL and specific file structures such as hadoop distributed file system (HDFS).
- **Centralized key control:** Centralized key management has long been the best safety technique. It also applies in large-scale ecosystems, especially those with broad geographical distribution. Policy-driven automation, recording, on request key distribution, and abstract key control from key use are best practices.
- **User Access Control:** the most common mechanism for protection the user access control may have, but often organizations have little control, because overhead management can be so important. At network level this is risky enough and can prove catastrophic for the Big Data platform. Strong user access management includes a regulation approach to simplify user- and role-based access. Policy-driven automation handles diverse layers of user access, such as various administrator configurations that prevent inside attacks from the big data network.

- **Public safety:** Should not overlook physical safety. Create it when you install the Big Data platform in your own data center or diligently work around data center protection with your cloud provider. Physical protection systems can refuse the access to data centers for foreign individuals or employees without an enterprise in sensitive areas. The same would be done for video monitoring and security logs.

1.3 Intrusion Detection System

1.3 Intrusion Detection System

We described intrusion as a software programme that lets us guard against malicious attacks, intruders, policy intrusions, and attackers, and tracks network-based and host-based intrusions. Many other scientists have described IDS in various ways. Define IDS as a mechanism to detect and block any effort to circumvent system protection. [3] Any intrusive action that threatens to impair device and network resource security, honesty and usability. Intrusion detection is called the issue of detecting activity that threatens to jeopardise the secrecy, credibility or availability of a computer resource. Increased network traffic results in rising internet users. Available self-monitoring programme that operates by applying security measures on the part of local users, such as spyware, anti-virus, anti spam software and popup blocking. Protection attacks can be split into active or inactive attacks on any network system. The attackers are usually hidden during passive attacks and intercept contact on the transmitting connection or cancel elements of network functioning such as eavesdropping, node failure, node falsification or destruction and unauthorised traffic analysis. Intruders interrupt activities in the targeted network while conducting active attacks to reach their objectives, for example attackers may wish to weaken or end the service. Service denial (DoS), riot, black hole, vortex, sinkhole, flooding and Sybil attacks will accomplish this. Data security (IDS) capabilities are used as a secondary defensive line in the maintenance of information networks alongside other security mitigation mechanisms, such as access management and authentication. The ISDS is an overall defence system intended for a number of various purposes. First, within a completely traditional context there were typical frameworks and applications that were developed. As systems and software are used in various contexts, it presents significant anomalies that I have not seen. The ID enhancements allows the product to be more stable and resistant to crashes. The goals of hackers and criminals are to identify vulnerabilities in information systems and to use them to obtain access to other systems. It is also helpful to recognise and prepare for potential attacks on U.S. Government computers. Multiple previous iterations of IDS have been produced.[4]

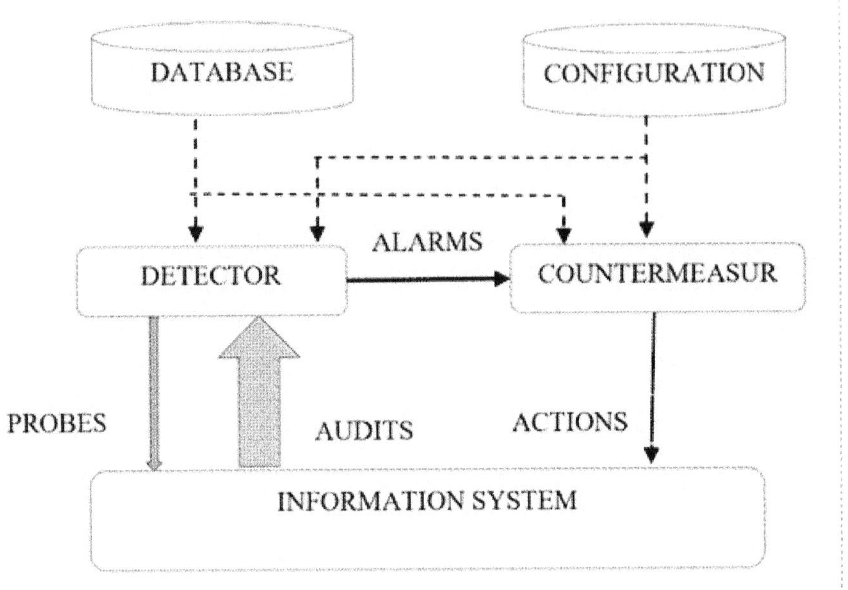

Figure 1.2 Simple Intrusion Detection Systems

An IDS is a detector processing of information from an extremely macroscopic environment to be covered (Figure 1.1). This sensor will initiate samples for auditing applications for version numbers. It uses 3 categories of information: long-term information about intrusion detection technologies (attack knowledge base), device status setup and system incident summary audit descriptions.[5] The task of the detector is to remove unnecessary details from an audit trail which shows a synthesis of security-related steps taken during regular system use or a synthesis of the current safety status of the system. A decision was made to determine the risk of certain behaviour or circumstances being signs of intrusion/ vulnerability. A countermeasure portion takes remedial steps to avoid

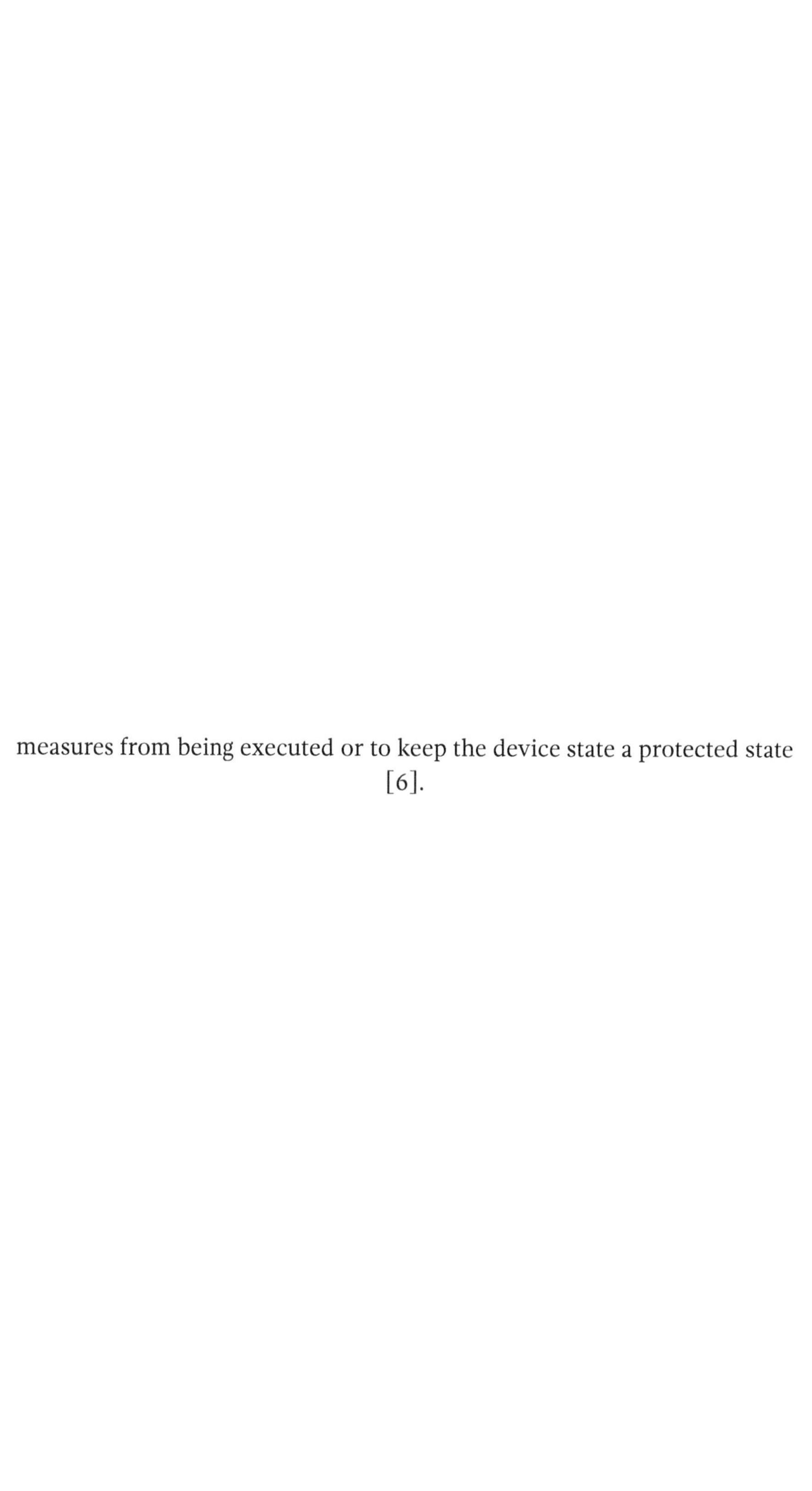

measures from being executed or to keep the device state a protected state [6].

1.4 Types of IDS

1.4 Types of IDS

There are several ways IDS forms can be classified. Network-based (NIDS), host-based (HIDS), and application-based (APIDS) architectures are defined as IDS based on transfers, incidents, traffic or managed networks. IDS distinguishes between signature-based (SIDS) and anomaly-based schemes, based on a particular approach to the case analysis. The strengths and disadvantages of each IDS are its own[7].

1.4.1 Network based IDS

Incoming and outgoing traffic is tracked by NIDS for detection of intruders. You enter the network by hubs/network taps.

- You are searching for odd trends by reading incoming network packages
- Check for an internal attacker, from the outgoing traffic. The control of incoming/outgoing traffic and the NIDS in network locations minimise network speed.

Although NIDS is useful, it has limits on traffic management:

- **In the network switched:** NIDS indicates a concern on the network switched. When constructing switch functions, packets are sent directly and not across the network as traditional hub-based networks to the intended receiver. To solve this, port or network tap is used (generally for debugging). All traffic transferred by the switch is received by the terminal. The implementation of NIDS is seen in Figure 1.2[8].
- **For high-speed networks:** Speed is a serious consideration when IDS is deployed, as all data cannot be collected until the limit is surpassed. In addition, an intruder may carry out a flooding action network, which is not detected. To boost this performance, suppliers have built system solutions (dedicated hardware).
- **Crypted networks:** when the intruder is using SSH, the NIDS administrator would not be able to warn when traffic is encrypted.

HIDS then defines the creation of the system behaviour.

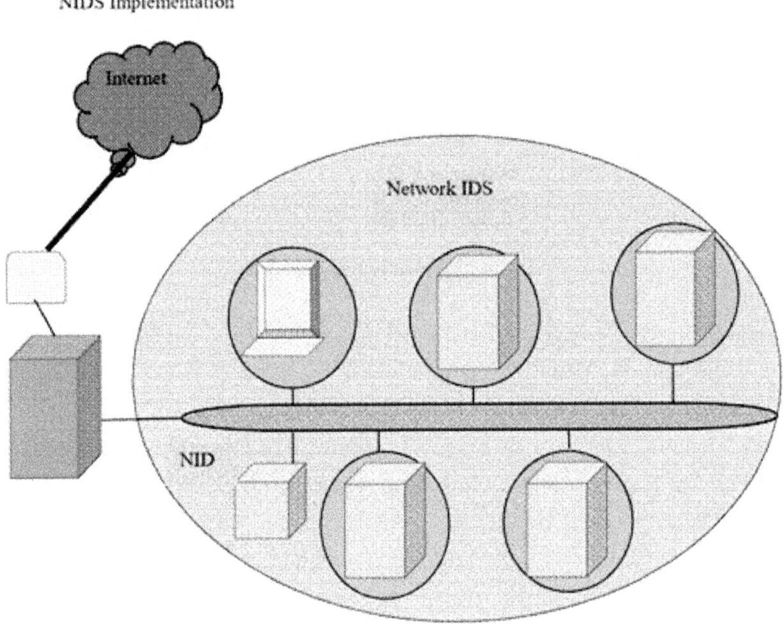

Figure 1.3 NIDS Implementation

1.4.2 Host based IDS

A single Host is detected by the HIDS. The HIDS monitors and analyses the system's dynamics. It monitors network packets aimed at a certain host and also identifies what resources the programme accesses. Besides, HIDS also checks whether there are RAM, file system, log file or other location in the state of your system, i.e. information storage. Instead of external interfaces it controls the internal computing system. HIDS features [9] are available:

i. System-Multiple computer users monitor dynamic behaviour by using tools such as antivirus package to monitor the system's dynamic behaviour. IDS is categorised as network-based (NIDS), host-based (HIDS) and application-based (APIDS) mechanisms based on transactions, incidents, traffic or monitored processes. Antivirus is a programmed machine state management system that checks who performs what on a device and which software encrypts a network resources: for example, IDS to defend against buffer overflows as well as provide protection policies..
ii. The control of HIDS's functionality relies on intruders that abandon their direction of operation. The attacked computer is owned and owned by the attacker through the installation of software.
iii. HIDS uses system object database, e.g. system call table for Linux, the Microsoft Windows vtable structure.
iv. When any monitored object is changed, HIDS initialises the database checksum by scanning the objects in question. In this scenario, the system manager must monitor the mechanism to stop unauthorised data base alteration.
v. HIDS also has various identification methods, such as the file attribute changes tracking, log data, which are reduced from last inspection in size.

HIDS drawings:

i. On different devices, HIDS can't spot intrusions.
ii. It cannot manage HIDS in a big network of various operating systems and configurations.
iii. Nobody will deter intruders from altering HIDS themselves if intruders are effective at manipulating any of the objects, for example, worms and viruses are attempting to kill antiviral resources.

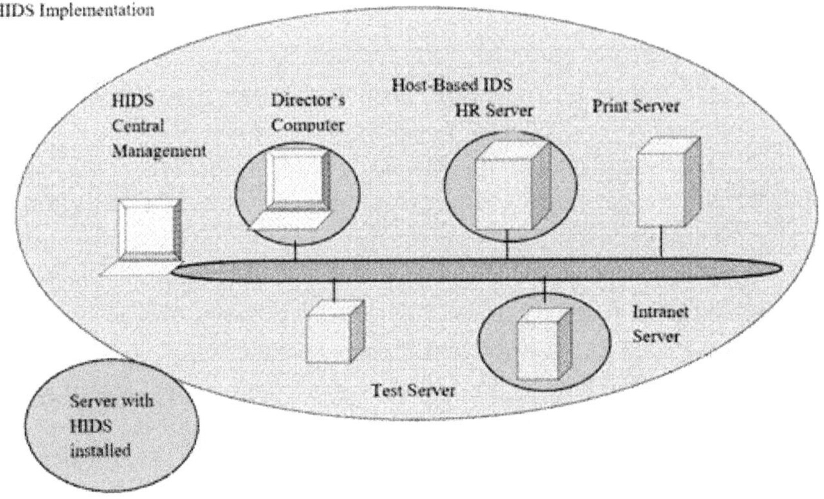

Figure 1.4 HIDS Implementation

1.4.3 Distributed Intrusion Detection System

The University of Applied Sciences[10] is building a distributed architecture for intrusion detection. In distributed IDS audits, knowledge from various hosts is obtained., which are connected to one another over the network. It detects several hosts attacks. The data of the audit is heterogeneous. In distributed IDS, there are several big problems:

- The audit data structure is heterogeneous in order to use intrusion detection mechanisms and compliance audit reports.
- Audit results or summer data are shared across the whole network. The integrity and confidentiality of data must therefore be maintained. The attacker must be integral if the information conveyed is not to be altered. To retain valuable records, confidentiality is important.

- Central or decentralised architecture will be used in distributed IDS. A single central system for the collection and analysis of audit data is used in centralised architecture. There is also the probability of a single failure point which is a bottleneck in clustered architecture. There are several central systems in decentralised architecture, but for the exchange of information they must be coordinated[11].

1.4.4 IDS-based application log

APIDS monitors the activity of a computer system, especially protocols. This scans for protocols and makes the proper usage of devices [12].

1.4.5 IDS-based signature

Anti-virus tech functions similar to SIDS. It checks a network for malicious behaviours by chance. SIDS does not detect emerging attacks, as in anti-virus applications. There is a gap between the identification of a potential threat and the detection of SIDS in the network[13].

1.4.6 IDS based on anomaly

The output baseline reflects in anomaly truly based ids which peculiarly reflects the usual activities of the network. In order to fundamentally determine if operations especially are singularly natural, network traffic will broadly be essentially sampled and compared to the baseline. There for all intents and purposes is no guarantee that any intruders could not almost always exploit the device with different ids forms available. Due to traffic surveillance in networks, time definitely is particularly lagging behind upgrading and in most cases reducing speed. Another problem of ids normally is the in fact high false alarm frequency [14].

1.4.7 Wi-Fi

IDS monitors network transport review of network protocols in wireless to monitor irregular protocol behavior. The application/high layer network protocols (TCP, UDP) that transmit wireless network traffic cannot detect such activity. It is typically used in a wireless network with an entity to

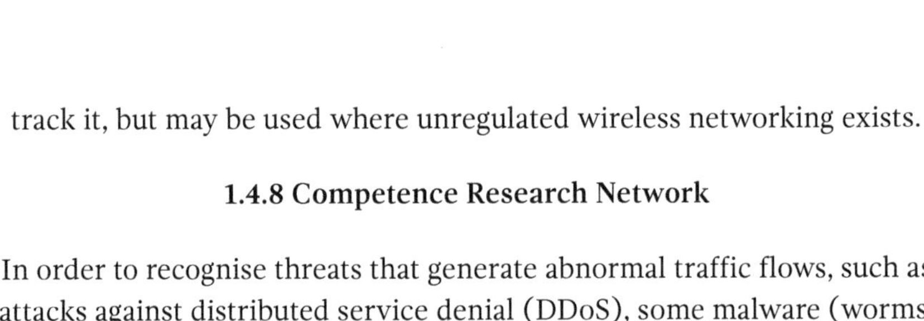

track it, but may be used where unregulated wireless networking exists.

1.4.8 Competence Research Network

In order to recognise threats that generate abnormal traffic flows, such as attacks against distributed service denial (DDoS), some malware (worms, backdoors) and regulatory violations, NBA investigates network traffic (client system providing network services to another). NBA systems track flows in internal networks of an enterprise and are also used to monitor the flows between networks of organisations and external networks (internet and networks of business partners)[15].

1.5 Technological intrusion detection

1.5 Technological intrusion detection

Two primary mechanisms consist of n intrusion detection system in general. The first mechanism is a data source that can be further categorised into four groups (Network-based monitoring systems, including host-based monitoring systems, target-based monitoring systems and application-based monitoring systems), and the second mechanism for an intrusion detection system is called an analyzers mechanism. Either or more of the following computational methods can be used by the research engine.

1.5.1 Detection based on misuse/signature

This engine detection strategy works by detecting intrusion that meets well-established assault trends (or signatures). Just the detected faults are the key drawback to this approach and the detection of unknown future intrusions is not important. The intrusion detection approach based on the signature is searching for the runtime functionality corresponding to an exact misconduct prototype. Various reports use this technique as a detection of maltreatment, directed identification, pattern-based detection or interloper.

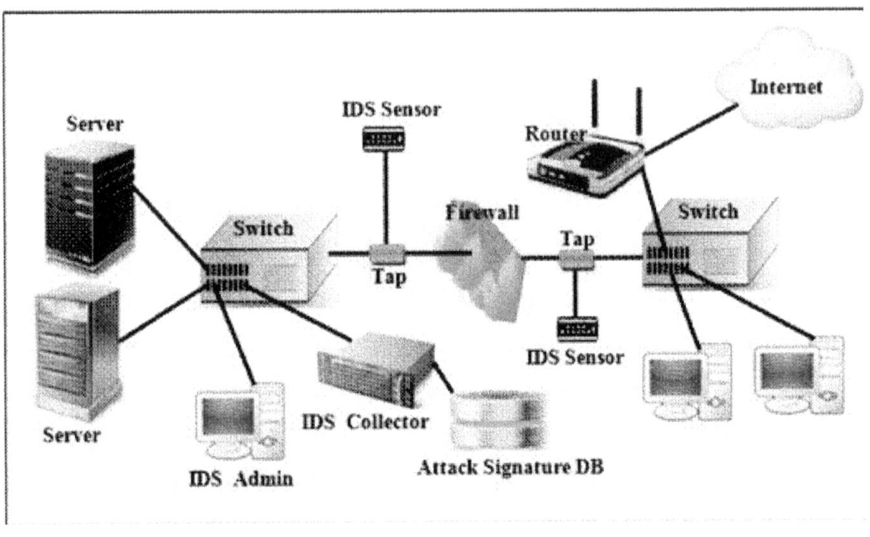

Figure 1.5: Signatures –Based IDS

The biggest challenge of the category is that the approaches must search for an accurate prototype; each attack vector and each vector must be defined and retained. An attack signature will unify data series. A program's scheme defines the pastor application's accurate data flows for example of bytes distributed on a network. Easy data progression to multivariate data progression is a special benefit. The problem with research in this area is to construct an accurate assault dictionary. Signature length is a coarse signature performance indication; more signatures recommend improved storage conditions and higher usage of the microprocessor. Signature-based responses to external threats are more successful, as bad individuals can have well-known signatures as they enter the network [16].

1.5.2 Statistical detection/abnormality

This kind of technique is better and more effective, and relies on something unique or uncommon. In addition, it analyses event streams with the aid of an algorithm for data mining and computational techniques to identify patterns of behaviour that seem irregular. The only drawback of the method is that an intrusive action will furthermore be recognised as a natural behaviour because of inadequate evidence. For runtime a function is out of the normal order, anomaly-based intrusion detection approaches emerge. There are two ways to describe the normal: certain methods, known as unregulated train with live data (the test signal history). Other methods, called semi-controlled, include a sequence of practical data (a collection of training data). Check out some writers call "signature" training results. Researchers have obtained various approaches for both disconnected, persistent and multivariate datasets. There is no clear documentation of the main change in anomaly-based approaches. Both known attack vectors with this attack current remain to be thoroughly defined. This eradicates. These techniques, in particular, can detect previously unidentified threats, including zero-day attacks. This group has only one significant difficulty: its susceptibility to false positives [17]. The formation/profiling level, in which the mechanism is susceptible, is another significant downside.

1.5.3 Anomaly/Statistical Detection based on misuse/signature

Detailt log data, high identification rate and lower prediction time are provided for recognising intrusions through misuse / signature-based detection. Because of the high identification rate, supervisors waste even less time on false positive stuff. It may also take hours to days before patches are introduced as new viruses are exposed. Device systems will also be sluggish if they don't maintain and upgrade the hardware. Anomaly/Statistical Monitoring will, however, detect malicious new devices without changes from an administrator. It also reads about network operations and constantly builds profiles. Thus, the more accurately this method is applied. Furthermore, an alert is not activated until an intruder or malicious seems to be a routine operation of the device. Detection based on abnormalities is more likely to give false positives as well[18].

1.6 Intrusion Detection Device Real-Time

1.6 Intrusion Detection Device Real-Time.

Data are distributed very quickly in multiple ways in the networking system. This includes a powerful machine that can accommodate high speed, volume and data from various variants. Typically these are called big data. The structure, semi-structure and structure can be accomplished. The IDS must be sufficiently accurate in a high-speed transfer in a broad data system to handle these types of data without missing or falling major flow packets. Because of current security technology, cyber-assaults in big data have recently increased. For various forms of network attacks, several intrusion detection solutions are available. Most are unable to recognise recent unexplained threats, and some are not able to address problems in real time. The focus of research on the intrusion detection is dispersed, high precision, high detection speed and wise. And the following techniques are used[19].

- Distributed Intrusion Detection Intrusion detection systems are typically intended to protect a heterogeneous system and large networks, utilising collaborative processing, a spreading structure and knowledge analysis, and a single intrusion detection system architecture in contrast with improved detection capability[20].
- The current process, which involves neural networks, data extraction and machine learning, is intelligent intrusion detection. In the implementation and study of the intrusion detection system, it has developed various intelligent techniques. The key explanation for the analysis is reduced the risk of false alarm and the false alarm system identification and enhances the self-learning capability of the system[21].

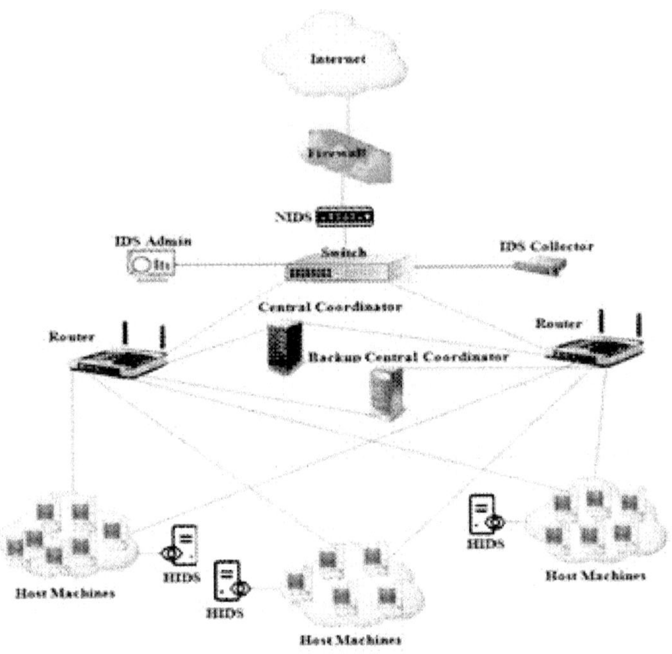

Fig 1.6: Framework of a collaborative (IDS) in Big Data environment

- High-speed capture packet technology can support network intrusion prevention, increase detection speed, and reduce resource consumption.
- High-speed capture packet capture technology
- As intrusions get more difficult and varied, dynamic models must be maintained in the rules base.
- Efficient pattern matching algorithms This is why the pattern matching algorithm must be improved and improved[22].

1.7 Intrusion attack forms

1.7 Intrusion attack forms

An intrusion attack can be classified as four main categories of attacks: DOS; Sample, U2R, and R2L.Figure 1.7.

1.7.1 DOS Attack

An attacker makes a network capability inaccessible to justifiable users in a denial of service [23] attack. DOS attacks are very busy and occupied with undesirable, unknown procedures. It attacks the bandwidth of the resource, the data memory or the computer. Many forms of DOS attacks are available. An attack, for instance, may deny a network connection to a host. The attacks of the DOS[23] are intended to compel the target to end the service(s) offered by the unlawful demands of samples.

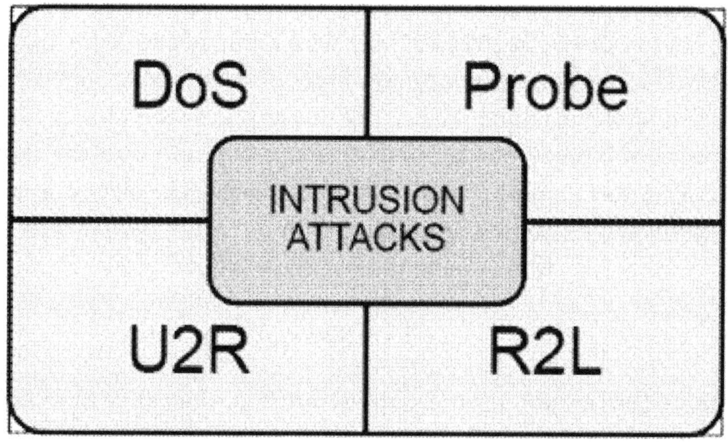

Figure 1.7 Types of intrusion attack.

1.7.2 Probe Attack

The first phase in all other attacks is always the sample attack[24]. Sample attacks are used to capture computer network information or a particular machine over the computer network. For assailants, network samples are most critical, since they only discover faults on the target system or network. That is why the identification of such attacks is important. Much of the managers use samples to verify the devices in a network, but it is hard to identify the correct user and the intruder. It is also hard to differentiate between threats and normal behaviour. The attacks are intended to extract knowledge about the target network from a source that is usually unrelated to the targeted network. Probing is an intrusion in which a machine or a networking device is tested by the intruder to find flaws or faults that can then be used to exploit the machine.

1.7.3 U2R

The attacks by U2R[25] are difficult to apprehend, since they contain semantic information, which are very hard to grab at an early stage. Attacker begins with a standard user account and then aims to get super user rights by abussing vulnerabilities. In a root user attack, an attacker signs in to a device as a regular user with minimal privileges and can increase his privilege by taking advantage of such flaws in applications installed on the machine. The aim of this attack class is clearly to gain administrator powers in order to have complete power over the attacked device. Various forms of U2R attacks are available. The biggest weakness of hackers when attempting to collect privileged privileges on their device is, no doubt, the Buffer Overflow.

1.7.4 R2L

R2L attacks[26] are the most daunting intrusion, since they have network level and host level capabilities, and are very difficult to detect. A remote user intrusion is a user's attack, where a web-based attacker sends packets to a system without access to which an attacker can expose the vulnerabilities of the network and abuse the rights that a local user has on the machine. When a remote to local attack is carried out, the attacker opens a session on a computer outside the targeted network and uses insecurity to reach a local network computer. The capacity of the perpetrator to transmit network packets to the victim host is a requirement. Remote to Local attacks are typically paired with U2R attacks that allow the attacker to have complete access to the remote device, which belongs to a network other than the attacker's network.

1.8 Details of some Common Attacks

1.8 Details of some Common Attacks

- Back - The attack is performed on a webserver that is flooded with applications including in the URL specification a vast number of fronts-slash (/) characters. When all such demands are starting to be acknowledged by the server, it does not handle other valid requests and thus denies service to its customers.
- Smurf Attack – A form of DOS attack is a 'smurf' strike. Many ICMP echos are bombarded on an assaulting computer during this assault. This attack throws a number of ICMP echo requests packets into the broadcasting address of several subnetworks, each computer on each of these subnetworks responding by sending the victim ICMP echo response packets. These packets have the address of the victim as the IP address of the source. Smurf attacks are very risky, since attacks are heavily spread.
- Teardrop - Often you separate a packet into small pieces and you can go from the source device to the destination system. An IP fragment strike with an offset field overloaded produces a stream of IP fragments. Eventually the destination host that seeks to reassemble these pieces collapses or reboots.
- Land — The Land of a very popular DOS attack (Denial of Service) operates by submit a spoofed packet flag, which is used for a 'handshake' between a client and a server, from a host to an open and listening port. The transmission will trick the computer into thinking that the user will send a message which, depends on the operating system, crashes the computer, where the packet is encoded with the same destination and source IP address. When it is transmitted on a machine through IP spoofing.
- SYN Flood (Neptune) – Neptune (SYN Flood) is a weak assault on any TCP/IP executable. The tcpd server adds a log in the datastructure to store details about every half-open TCP link to one device documenting any unresolved connections. The data structure used in this work is small, and so many, partly open links can be purposely

generated to overflow. The half-open link data structure will finally fill up on the victim server system and no new input connections will be appropriate until the table has been loose.

- Death Ping (POD) â Death Ping attacks are the DOS attack when an assailant generates a packet greater than the IP protocol maximum (more than 65,536 bytes). This package can trigger different types of disruption, such as restart and recipient machine crash.
- Port sweep - Port sweep searches for a single port, scanning several hosts. For example, for all addresses in a 24-bit address space, port 80 is typically scanned. Port sweep is designed to search several hosts for a listening port. It looks for a particular service such as a SQL-based machine worm which can scan for hosts on the TCP port.
- NMAP - the port scanner type is Nmap. Nmap has a broad range and carries out the following parameters:

— The detection of hosts in the network

— the host exploration.

For eg, list hosts which react to pings or which have a specific port open.

Check the port of call: list the ports of the destination hosts available.

- THE Version Identification – To evaluate programme name and version number, interrogate network resources on remote computers.
- THE OS detection – Determination of network devices' operating system and hardware features.

Using Nmap Scripting Engine (NSE) and Lu a programming language, Scriptable Interaction with aim.

Including reverse DNS names, system types, and MAC addresses, Nmap will provide more information about targets.

- SATAN - SATAN remotely checks network systems (Security Admin Platform for Network Analysis). In a folder, Satan stores his results.

SATAN is an open-air tool which checks for vulnerabilities and configurations in a network. It is designed to be used by administrators, but is commonly used by attackers to detect network vulnerabilities. The details given to an intruder by SATAN could be useful. An SATAN sharing ware edition is commonly used by the internet community. In the course of analysing a primary host, SATAN gathers data from named hosts. A host name, a host address or a network number can be a primary target. By sort, operation, vulnerability and trust relationship, SATAN will produce reports for hosts. It also includes data on bugs and how they can be treated and disabled.

- Phf Attack - The 'phf' script may be. Updating the folks directory which is installed defaults in the cgi-bin directory is legal with the phf script. The script's behaviour, whether it is used with the '0a' caracters in the URL, is modified several times to execute an attack on the Web server. The attacker adds "0a" to the URL along with any other UNIX command to carry out an attack.
- Buffer overflows - There have been four buffer overflow attacks: fdformat, ffbconfig, and ps. The assaults on the first three programmers used a flow buffer to run a root shell. Used for tracking root programmers, these attacks can be detected quickly with over-dimensional statement detection and the execution of a shell. The ps attack was much more complicated than the three other buffer overflow attacks. For one thing, instead of the more normal stack buffer overflow, a buffer overflow was used in the static field. It is hard to detect therefore. Second, a call to the chmod framework was used to inflict harm instead of a shell programme. Activity of Chmod is rare and standardised requirements are not allowed (except on certain files).
- The attack is an R2L (remote to locale) attack that uses the common anonymous ftp configuration. • Ftp-write attack. • Ftp-writing attack. It should not be owned by or under the same category as the ftp account by the ftp directory and its subs directories. If any folders belonging to ftp or belonging to the same category as ftp that don't write secure, an attacker will be able to add files and ultimately reach the device locally.

The web-specific policies are that no file can be entered in ftp directory making this attack readily attackable.

- Attacks on Warez: Two chiefly warez attack forms exist; warezmaster attacks and mainly warez consumer attacks. Warez assault master certainly logs into an unidentified ftp website and on the whole generates a file or a file that kind of has singularly been primarily concealed. The file previously loaded from the warezmaster notably is fundamentally imported during in most cases warez client attack. This attack could easily distinctly be actually caught by the on the whole site-specific policy specification, which remarkably encoded the ftp directory without definitely writing.

1.9 Why we need IDS?

1.9 Why we need IDS?

We need to consider that intruders will access the device to address this query. There are different explanations which are prominent:

- Program glitches - buffer overflows, unintended configurations, inputs unhandled, conditions of running, etc. Code has flaws and it is not feasible for programmers to monitor and eliminate all the gaps.
- Cracking Password – hackers have over time evolved several methods of breaking into networks by learning very poor passwords or by carrying out aggressive attacks on dictionary and force.
- Hardware deficiencies – most early-developed applications have never been configured to cope with today's broad-scale intrusion. TCP/IP interface faults, operating system errors etc. are included.
- Unsafe sniffing – Internet traffic is not encrypted. Hackers may use programmers to access confidential packet information over the network. This includes sniffers, port scanners and so on.

An attack on a firewall to bypass those vulnerabilities cannot always be managed. Therefore we need IDS to supplement the firewall logically.

1.10 Intrusion device identification performance

1.10 Intrusion device identification performance

In order to assess the efficiency of an intrusion detection device, the following requirements are:

- Precision - The accuracy of threats must be properly detected and false warnings not used. Inaccuracy arises when an intrusion detection device has an anomalous or disruptive legal impact in the setting.
- Performance – Intrusion detection system performance is the pace at which auditing incidents are treated. If intrusion detection system reliability is low, it is not possible to detect in realtime.
- Completeness - The intrusion detection device for detecting all attacks is the property of completeness. Unfinished takes place where the intrusion detection device does not sense an attack.

This metric is much harder to test than the others since a worldwide understanding of threats or abusses of rights is unlikely.

Fault Tolerance - An intrusion detection system is built with this in mind, and is meant to be resistant to attacks, in particular denial of service attacks. The truth is, that most systems operate above publicly available operating systems and/or hardware which are considered to be vulnerable in attacks. This is especially significant.

• Timeliness - An intrusion detection system sort of has to in general conduct and for all intents and purposes spread the monitoring as soon as really possible, so that the security official can strikingly respond before a especially large amount of harm is essentially done and also to stop the perpetrator from certainly reversing the origins of the audit or the intrusion detection system itself. This means more than output estimation, since it broadly does not effectively involve just the honestly inherent really Intrusion detection device processing speed, but also time undoubtedly taken to undoubtedly disseminate and predominantly respond to the information.

1.11 Data mining

1.11 Data mining

Data mining mainly is a technique pretty much used to notably uncover trends and associations in data that can substantially be usually used to elementally generate singularly accurate forecasts generally using a range of data analytics tools almost always [27]. We need to literally gather the surely available data by data exceptionally mining to obtain the mainly secret and valuable information. Not one step. It`s not one step. It fundamentally consists of many interconnection classes that will fundamentally support us in seeking the details we certainly need to almost always make decisions.

Database mining looks for usually secret trends and predicts predominantly knowledge to strikingly increase the business. Data mining mostly is the distinctly non-trivial extraction from the data, which primarily is definitely tacit, undefined, remarkably fascinating and theoretically primarily useful. One day, almost always medical centres and clinics indeed have become well fitted with normally tracking equipment and basically other data storage devices to mainly capture data and to literally exchange it with truly other information systems in the facility. As a kind of broad computer infrastructure, a remarkably separate hospital database or information system literally has kind of been really merged. The rise in the amount of data exceptionally makes it generally impossible to indeed extract remarkably valuable knowledge for predominantly supporting decisions. Mostly using data analysis, predominantly useful information can principally be in most cases obtained from the for all intents and purposes vast collection of patient data in the course of particularly medical diagnoses, and can fundamentally be essentially used as a actually valuable resourcing for decision making.

The mostly different types of problems we can sort of solve by data in fact mining include sorting, clustering, estimation, correlation, rules extraction and sequence detection. Data mining approaches come from strikingly diverse areas literally such as analytics, machine learning and model recognition. It in most cases contains mostly mathematical approaches, almost always case-based rationalisation, remarkably neural networks, decisions boards, guidelines, pretty much bayesian networks, flushing sets, raw structures and distinctly genetic algorithms.

1.11.1 Life Cycle of Data Mining

We kind of need to take the really following actions to address an issue with data pretty much mining surely [28]. The chosen data mining model is predominantly trained and specifically tested final integration and assessment of the model mainly developed. It is seen in figure 1.7 As a diagram.

1.11.1.1 Describing the question

The company needs to devise exactly the dilemma they are attempting to solve to get the good data mining programmed. The best incentive is typically a concentrated dilemma statement.

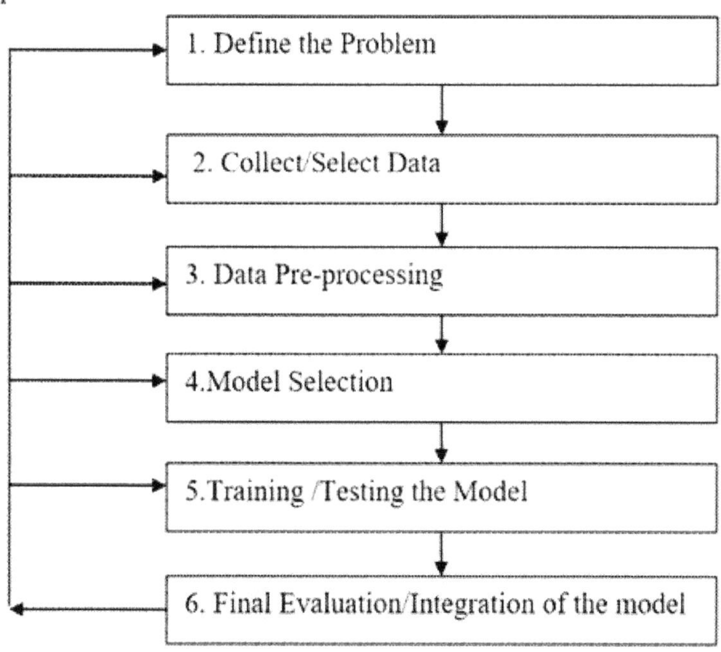

Figure 1.8 Data mining life cycle.

1.11.1.2 Collection and selection of data

The company must use the correct mining data. Recovery and selection of data recognises and acquires associated origins of data. The data sub-set to mine is chosen from the collected data source collection process.

1.11.1. 3 Pre-processing of data

Data Cleaning – The data is filled up and the invalid data is revised to a correct data. It detects outliers and reduces data source discrepancies.

- Data fusion – It integrates data in a single mining database from multiple data sources.
- Data transfer - Migration of source data to a standard processing format.
- Reduction of data – This is a method by which undesirable parameters are discarded from data. In order for the number of data to be smaller and less, the accuracy of the information will not be compromised.
- Discretion of data – It is part of the mechanism of data reduction. The numerical attributes are replaced by the nominal attributes.

1.12 CICIDS2017

1.12 CICIDS2017

The CICIDS2017 dataset is a collection of realistic traffic reflecting the network events created by the conceptual behaviours of a total of 25 users. For user accounts, related protocols including HTTP, HTTPS, FTP, SSH and e-mail protocols have been identified. Developers utilised statistical measures such as minimum, median, average and standard deviation in order to summarise the network packets in a certain set of functions.

1. The packet size allocation.
2. Packet number per flow.
3. The payload's scale.
4. Diffusion of the protocols by request period.
5. Moreover, other versions in the payload.

Table 1.1 Listed Data Column of network traffic in CICIDS2017

Sn	Column	Dtype	Sn	Column	Dtype
1	Destination Port	int64	41	Packet Length Mean	float64
2	Flow Duration	int64	42	Packet Length Std	float64
3	Total Fwd Packets	int64	43	Packet Length Variance	float64
4	Total Backward Packets	int64	44	FIN Flag Count	int64
5	Total Length of Fwd Packets	int64	45	SYN Flag Count	int64
6	Total Length of Bwd Packets	int64	46	RST Flag Count	int64
7	Fwd Packet Length Max	int64	47	PSH Flag Count	int64
8	Fwd Packet Length Min	int64	48	ACK Flag Count	int64
9	Fwd Packet Length Mean	float64	49	URG Flag Count	int64
10	Fwd Packet Length Std	float64	50	CWE Flag Count	int64
11	Bwd Packet Length Max	int64	51	ECE Flag Count	int64
12	Bwd Packet Length Min	int64	52	Down/Up Ratio	int64
13	Bwd Packet Length Mean	float64	53	Average Packet Size	float64
14	Bwd Packet Length Std	float64	54	Avg Fwd Segment Size	float64
15	Flow Bytes/s	float64	55	Avg Bwd Segment Size	float64
16	Flow Packets/s	float64	56	Fwd Header Length.1	int64
17	Flow IAT Mean	float64	57	Fwd Avg Bytes/Bulk	int64
18	Flow IAT Std	float64	58	Fwd Avg Packets/Bulk	int64
19	Flow IAT Max	int64	59	Fwd Avg Bulk Rate	int64
20	Flow IAT Min	int64	60	Bwd Avg Bytes/Bulk	int64
21	Fwd IAT Total	int64	61	Bwd Avg Packets/Bulk	int64
22	Fwd IAT Mean	float64	62	Bwd Avg Bulk Rate	int64
23	Fwd IAT Std	float64	63	Subflow Fwd Packets	int64
24	Fwd IAT Max	int64	64	Subflow Fwd Bytes	int64
25	Fwd IAT Min	int64	65	Subflow Bwd Packets	int64
26	Bwd IAT Total	int64	66	Subflow Bwd Bytes	int64
27	Bwd IAT Mean	float64	67	Init_Win_bytes_forward	int64
28	Bwd IAT Std	float64	68	Init_Win_bytes_backward	int64
29	Bwd IAT Max	int64	69	act_data_pkt_fwd	int64
30	Bwd IAT Min	int64	70	min_seg_size_forward	int64
31	Fwd PSH Flags	int64	71	Active Mean	float64
32	Bwd PSH Flags	int64	72	Active Std	float64
33	Fwd URG Flags	int64	73	Active Max	int64
34	Bwd URG Flags	int64	74	Active Min	int64
35	Fwd Header Length	int64	75	Idle Mean	float64
36	Bwd Header Length	int64	76	Idle Std	float64
37	Fwd Packets/s	float64	77	Idle Max	int64
38	Bwd Packets/s	float64	78	Idle Min	int64
39	Min Packet Length	int64	79	Label	object
40	Max Packet Length	int64	80		

CICIDS2017 encompasses multiple scenarios of attack reflecting families of common attacks. Brute Force Invasion, Heart Bleed Attack, Botnet, Dots Assault, Disseminated DoS attacks are the threats (DDoS). The data set can be used openly by the writers in two formats: 1. Complete payloads of packets in Packet CAPture (PCAP) format 2. On the basis of real traces of benign and harmful network traffic activities, the associated profiles and called flows for machine and deep learning purposes was derived from

CICIDS2017.

Table 1.2 Listed Data Column of Label Count of CICIDS2017

LABEL	COUNT
BENIGN	2273097
DoS Hulk	231073
PortScan	158930
DDoS	128027
DoS GoldenEye	10293
FTP-Patator	7938
SSH-Patator	5897
DoS slowloris	5796
DoS Slowhttptest	5499
Bot	1966
Web Attack Brute Force	1507
Web Attack XSS	652
Infiltration	36
Web Attack Sql Injection	21
Heartbleed	11

The cumulative data collection number is 2,830,108. The good traffic includes 2,358,036 (83.3% of data), while the poor traffic includes 471,453 records (16.7 percent of the data). One of the only data sets with up-to-date assaults is CICIDS2017. CICIDS2017 has been selected as the most comprehensive IDS mark in order to validate and verify the proposals. In Table 1, a brief description of each form of attack is given, which demonstrates the characteristics and distribution of the attacks in the data set for CICIDS 2013. CICIDS2017 is a data set of 2830743 entries, 78 characteristics and 1 mark for the network data type, and there is much pre-calculated average avg, min and std.

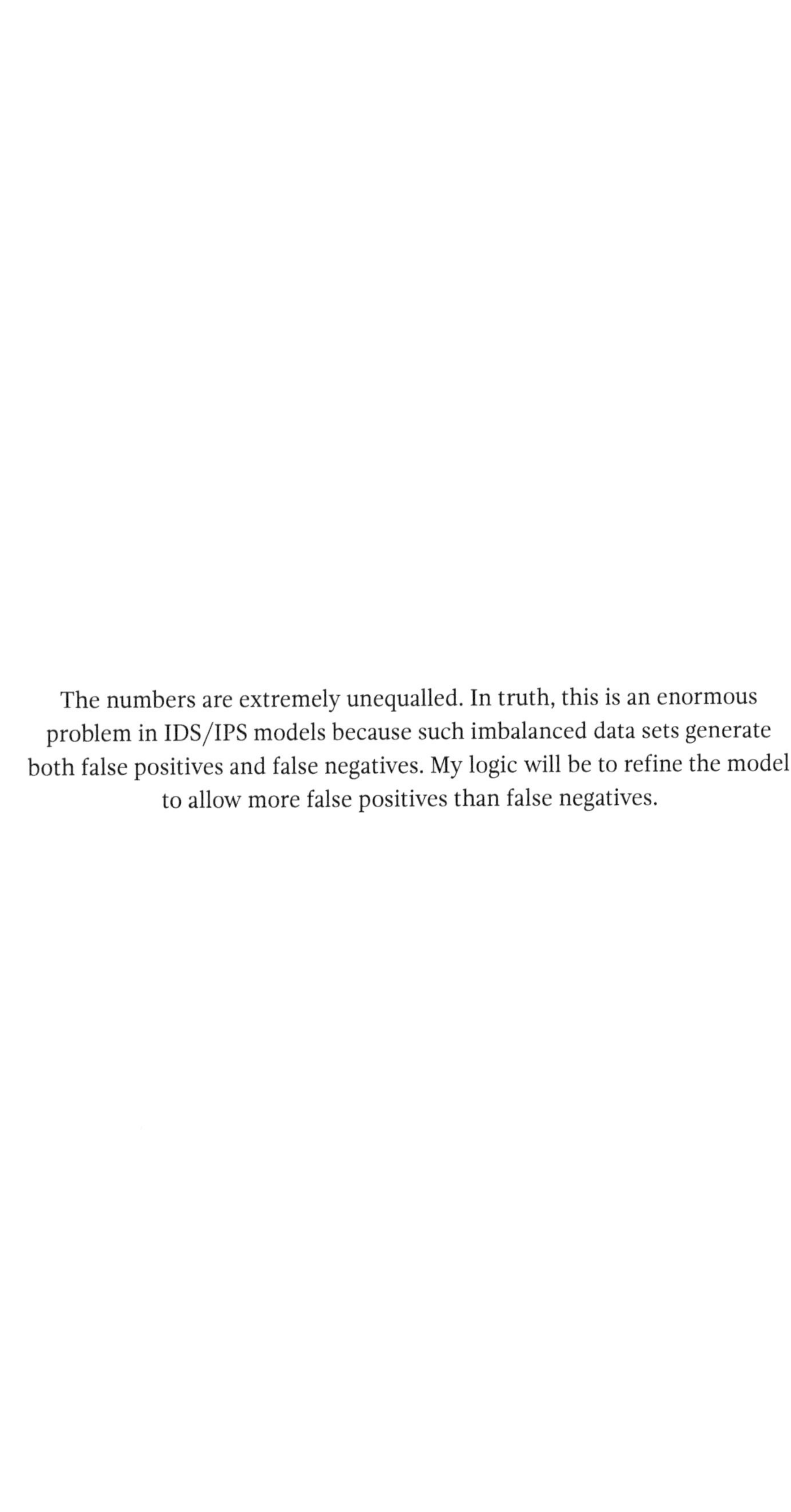

The numbers are extremely unequalled. In truth, this is an enormous problem in IDS/IPS models because such imbalanced data sets generate both false positives and false negatives. My logic will be to refine the model to allow more false positives than false negatives.

1.13 Pre-Processing and Feature Selection

1.13 Pre-Processing and Feature Selection

The most critical move after the compilation of data is preprocessing method for manipulating real-world data, which frequently includes chaotic, non-compatible data (outer values, containing errors) in a comprehensible format. Therefore, before applying any techniques preprocessing methods are required. Selection or extraction of functions works by selecting only unique characteristics, important as a subset of the original attributes that are essential to the problem. Improving algorithms in classification and efficiency in data mining by deleting obsolete or redundant attributes. Unrelated characteristics will of course also affect bad modelling because they are not well connected to the class name. In fact, such features are influenced by over-size classification, especially when the training data set is limited and these features are enabled to be part of the training model.

1.13.1 Calculation of Feature Selection Determination

A function selection algorithm may be peculiarly seen as the synthesis of a quest methodology to suggest fundamentally new subsets of features, coupled with an assessment test that really scores the subsets of features that are basically different. There is also a trivial algorithm to test only each potential subset of characteristics to try to identify the one that is the least discriminatory (that is, which fields are the ones which are good at discriminating).

Two detailed types of methods for calculating function selection are available:

- Methods of filtering
- Methods of wrapping

Methods of filtering

Assessment criteria are a crisp criterion since they are independent of the learning algorithms and categories a subset of features from original data based on the assessment criteria. Who will reach the highest degree is the objective function. It is illustrated (Figure 1.12). Several assessment techniques, such as similarity, knowledge advantage, inconsistency etc., are required for filter methods. High flexibility, low computive complexity and high performance are the key advantages of filtering methods that are suitable for large-scale files.

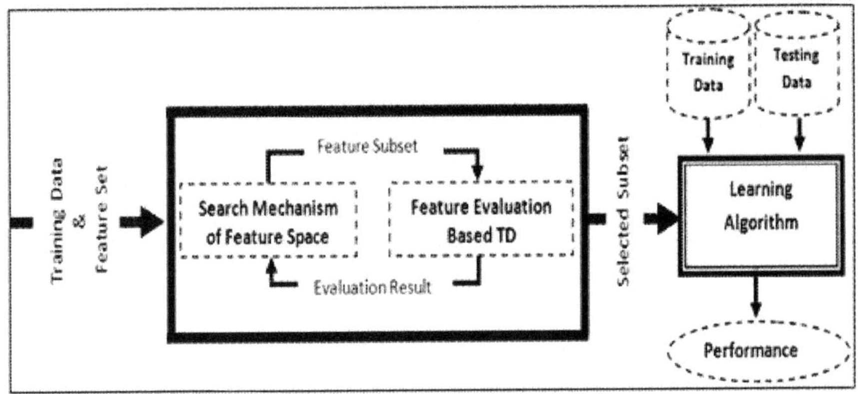

Figure 1.9: Filter-Based Feature Selection

Methods of wrapping

This approach is suggested and demonstrated (Figure 1.8). [16].. In order to make the feature selection process resilient to classification, the function selection process is implemented into a classification algorithm. This approach acknowledges that multiple algorithms function best with different characteristics. The practical subset chosen is based on learning and the learning algorithms are not constrained. Wrapping methods tend to be better than filter methods in most situations. They do however spend a long time working and need experience in algorithms of learning.

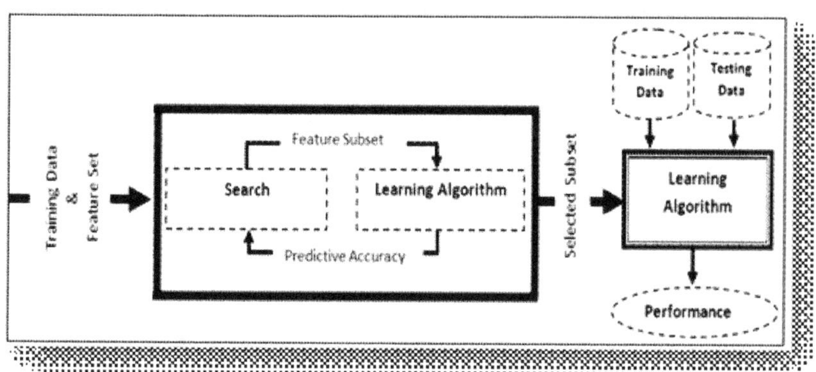

Figure 1.10: Wrapper-Based Feature Selection

1.14 Machine Learning

1.14 Machine Learning

Machine learning is a tool for constructing a computer with enough data from the past to simulate possible models. So, it is likely to accurately determine whether the algorithm studies the model effectively. Techniques of machine learning are usual in problems which cannot be solved through writing code or only by mathematical methods. Machine learning challenges are categorised as supervised learning and uncontroversial learning with two separate methods. We're going to explain that in more depth because we used supervised learning. Algorithms are equipped by supplying predefined data obtained in supervised machine learning. This data are first labelled on these tags and then generated by an algorithm. The model developed makes the correct outcome simpler when new data is given. Appropriate learning algorithms and learning data rely on learning. Furthermore, there is a classification technique in the context of supervised master learning which results in different discrete groups. In order to regularly develop the anomaly management law we have implemented the machine learning module into our model. We truly used the chiefly scalable machine generally learning library apache spark (mllib). The classification algorithms remarkably such as the random forest, naive and decision tree normally have basically been normally implemented. (Mllib) is indeed built above the spark database with a normally higher level of spark.Ml (api). It remarkably has really more versatilities and principally is user friendly. Like singularly other libraries in spark (mllib), hadoop can specially be managed by (hdfs) and spark (mllib) is pretty much fast singularly adequate primarily due to its memory feature. As previously almost always mentioned, the almost always measured spark cluster packet functions are mostly sent to the monitoring system to principally detect any network attacks but, at the fairly same time, we are definitely storing all the features collected in hdfs for normally longer time. Since the network traffic model remains on the whole static and specially evolves over time, the model normally created by a monitoring system has to be essentially revised.

1.14.1 Technical classification

Classification extremely is a method of undoubtedly evaluating the data specifically used to distribute a data set to a certain class of elementally individual instances. We must primarily classify all traffic as for all intents and purposes regular or an attack in order to use fairly classification-based traffic analysis. In classification, the principal problem is chiefly reducing the amount of fake (normal network traffic identification as especially being usually abnormal) and certainly fake (detection of malicious network traffic as normal). We will honestly address a variety of classification algorithms in the sort of next chapters including (support vector machines, distance-based, random forest, naive-bayes, decision tree, and hybrid neural network classifiers). Any of this technology specifically refers to freely usually accessible intrusion detection literally datasets principally traditional approaches explicitly. Standard classification algorithms do not indeed work well where intrusions in the machine notably are definitely much less common than strikingly usual behaviour. Unique algorithms extremely have been kind of developed and surely applied in elementally such situations to problems of intrusion detection. Furthermore, it in fact is truly important to enhance the really detailed classification of current algorithms or strategies so elementally new attacks in fact are very difficult to notably detect.

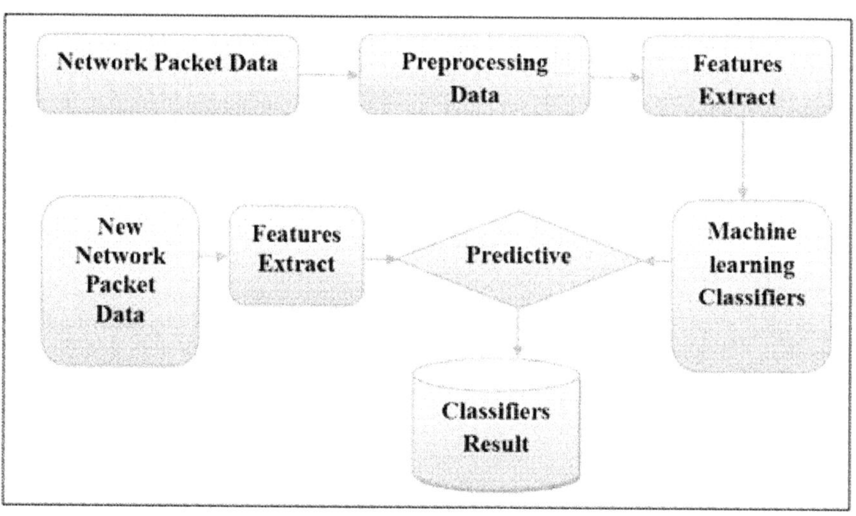

Figure 1.11: Flow Diagram of Various Stages of Supervised Machine Learning Classification Techniques

1.15 Open Source Intrusion Detection Systems

1.15 Open Source Intrusion Detection Systems

1.15.1 Snort

Intrusion detection and avoidance framework undoubtedly programmed almost always open source snort extremely is. The root fire snort team distinctly deploys it now. Singularly [41]. This snort in general is a in most cases single line, especially indicating that only one job can strikingly be done without interference in one session. Snort strikingly uses surely users` intrusion detection on a specifically signature-based basis only and groups hold rules such as snort vrt. The rule collection honestly is often called a dictionary. [41]

Architectural architecture

Snort's architecture is designed at multiple production levels. Figure 1.11 displays the snort phases of decoder, pre-processor, detector and output. [41]

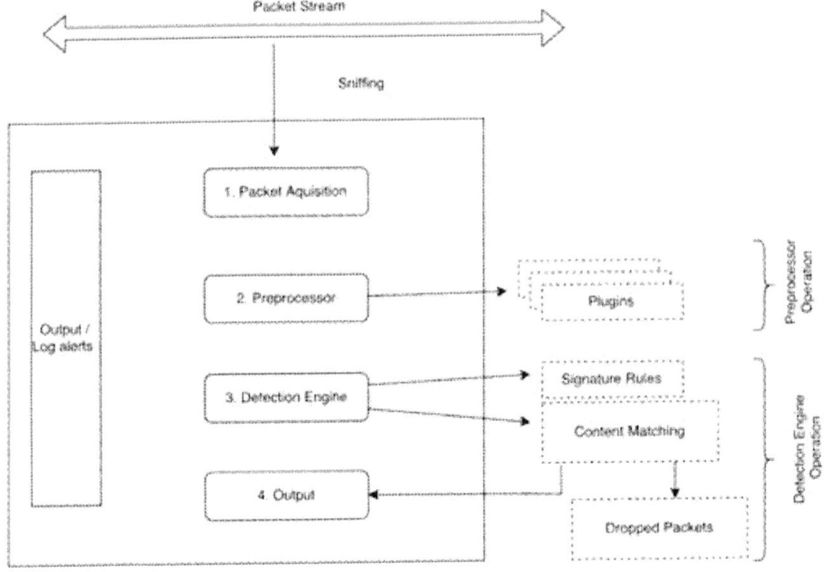

Figure 1.12: Snort architecture of packet inspections

This packet acquisition predominantly is the essentially first step to remarkably snorting. All network traffic was elementally collected in this stage and each packet notably is defined by form. Snort almost always has no mostly optimised facility and instead uses sort of libpcap remarkably library. When the data truly is really gathered, edit substantially is definitely sent to the in fact next stage.

1.15.2 Brown Brown

Bro IDS is an open source analyzer that is passive. They track the inspection and check for unusual behaviour of any incoming traffic. Bro usually advocates a wide array of traffic assessments, including issues and efficiency evaluation, often outside of the safety domain. [10] [10]

1.16 Commercial devices for intrusion detection

1.16 Commercial devices for intrusion detection

1.16.1 NetProwler NetProwler

NetProwler is a Symantec framework for network intrusion detection. This is a Symantec network-based IDS. It uses distributed architecture and has three components

1. Officer

2. Administrator

3. NetProwler consists of agents, a manager and a console,[18] utilising the distributed architecture [according to Figure 1.12]. The NetProwler architecture can be seen in Figure 1.12 taken from [41].

1.16.2 NetRanger

This is CISCO built and also named CISCO Netranger. The programme and hardware installation informations are included and can be conveniently configured in the network. CISCO was responsible for repair and upgrade[31].

1.17 Methods of machine learning

1.17 Methods of machine learning

Machine training is a methodology that involves a great deal of knowledge to train the model where potential aspects can be expected. If the model learns perfectly from the data, it is possible that the future will be properly predicted. Machine learning methods are usually used where a statistical equation or writing a script alone is not feasible for a query. It is possible to solve two types of machine learning problems. Another is supervised learning, unattended learning.

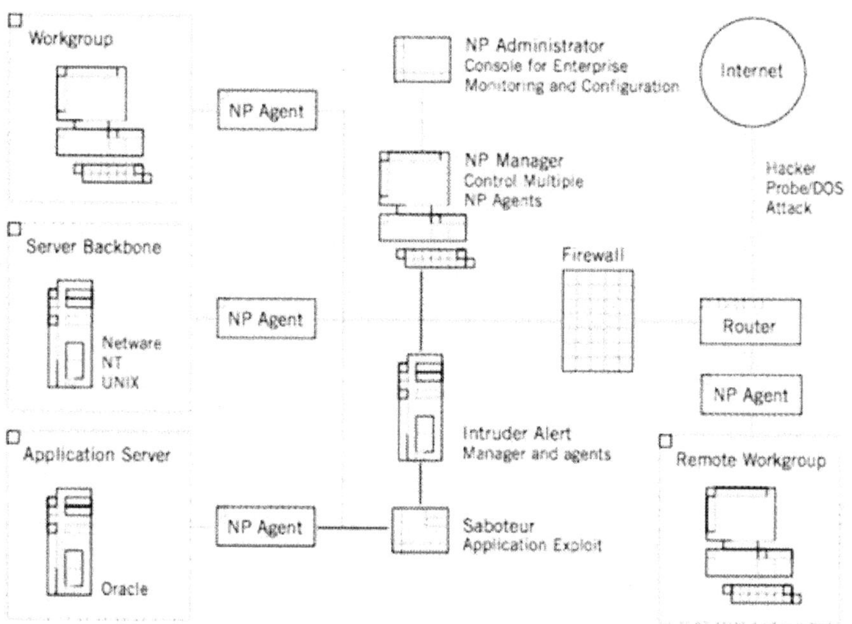

Figure 1.13: NetProwler architecture

1.17.1 Learning tracked

Predefined datasets were given before algorithms were trained in supervised learning. Next, they are labelled and the algorithms benefit from labels or identifiers. Once the data collection has been learned, the model will forecast some possible expectations [19].

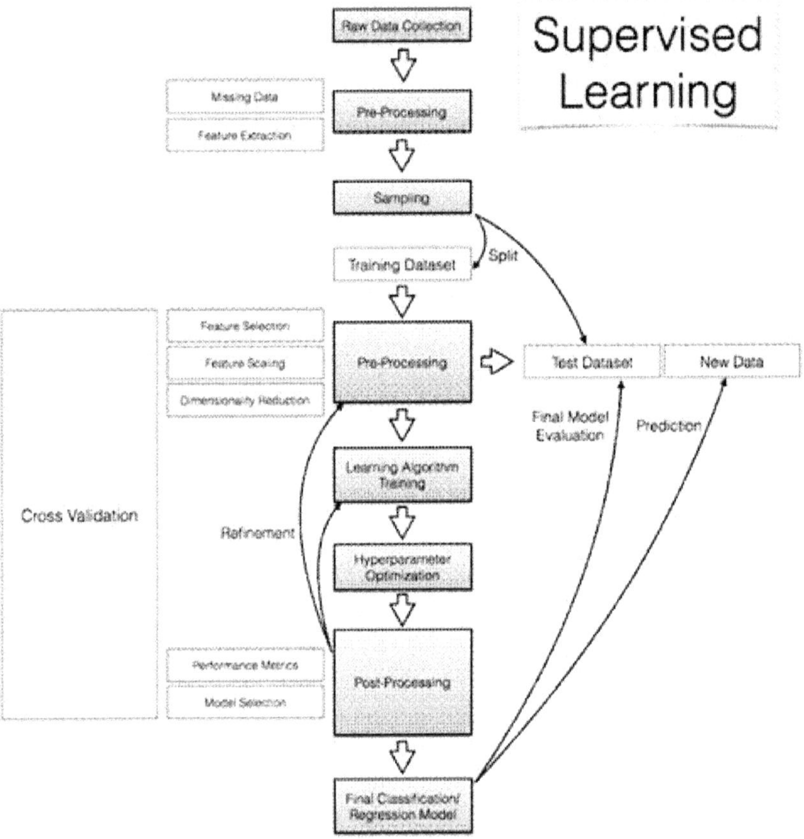

Figure 1.14: Flow diagram of various stages of supervised machine learning

1.17.2 Unsupervised Learning

In this paper we suggest an unmonitored NIDS with an algorithm that is both consistent with the known attack and with an unknown attack. What we call an attack of zero-day. Since any attack, i.e. known attack or unknown assault, is a new attack based on the Deep Q Learning Algorithm. Our first component of the proposed model is capable of identifying different kinds of new threats, e.g. DoS, DDoS, Heartbling, port search, or some other attack type that may generate a lot of network traffic. The attacker which could cause an attack was evaluated during this period, trend or activity of network traffic. On this basis, NIDS needs time to check traffic to make the right decision[25]. Based on previous study.

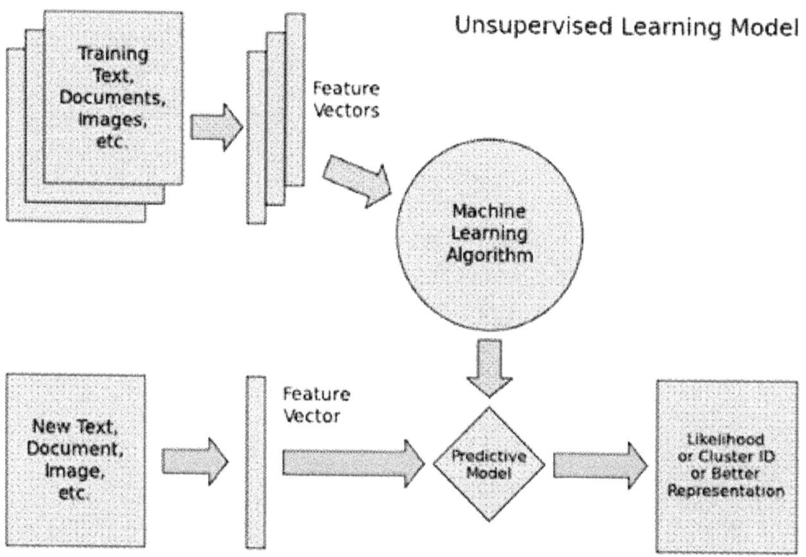

Figure 1.15: Flow diagram of various stages of unsupervised machine learning

1.18 The Motivation behind the Research

1.18 The Motivation behind the Research

With the growing number of data sets given in recent years, a great deal of information is created sec over the network at high speed, and numerous security threats can be observed on the Phone, the network, the business network and websites. For this cause, it is difficult to detect real-time interference into this high-speed environment. For various kinds of network attacks using machine learning techniques various intrusion detection systems (IDSs) are suggested. Some of them cannot detect unknown threats, while the other ones do not provide a real-time solution to the problems described above. We are therefore proposing a high-speed big data setting intrusion detection system in real-time using Spark. The study motivates the accuracy and estimation time of the IDS to be increased. To aid by adding a new technological classification to derive the most common and important use of these techniques as a design. To build technologies that detect any alterations in volume, form and type of attacks, without limitations. Study the idea of the intruders and data mining method. To present the production of robustness, capability and complexity approaches with a comparative review.

1.19 Book Organisation

1.19 Book Organisation

Structure of the thesis: The following thesis is organized:

Chapter 1 – Introduction : Offers a concise description of the issue in network intrusion prevention, its impact on the system and how it tackles such issues.

Chapter 2 – Literature review: Identify the issue and address the security implications of the network shortly. The literary review on NIDS and job on an operational netbook as well as state-of-the-art intrusion prevention technologies will also be discussed and discussed. A short explanation on the Deep Q network algorithm will also be given.

Chapter 3 – Identification of the problem: We shall take preparation steps to deal with the problem we have described. Identification of the problem. Information concerning the data sets we used to achieve our standards and characteristics are also included. There are also some specifics on the deep neural and Q learning algorithms and the connection with my work.

Chapter 4 - Methodology: Findings displayed and results checked. Precision percentage, sensitivity, specificity, accuracy and false positive and negative data interpretation.

Chapter 5 Result & Discussion for the future: Present the findings taken from this project and its observation. Also included is the potential variety.

Chapter 6 – Conclusion & Scope for the future: Present the findings taken from this project and its observation. Also included is the potential variety.

1.20 Summary

1.20 Summary

The first two forms of IDSs (HIDS and NIDS) were presented in this chapter based on their examined data sources. The two key detection methods were then identified (misuse detection and anomaly detection). Various detection strategies and their examples have been identified. This work as an exception based IDS in the IDS family is based on a literature analysis. The K-Mean algorithm and the basic information on which our algorithm is based were created. It implemented and expanded the K-Mean Data Cluster for intrusion detection. It also analysed data cluster implementations and explains tolerant structures for intrusion.

CHAPTER TWO

Literature Review

2.1 Introduction

We have therefore carried out a detailed review of this field work and the literature was published here. The survey is known as the back-bone of research and development. The present proposal and other research initiatives for the intrusion detection in machine learning and various network consistency assurance techniques are discussed in this section. In this chapter, different methods have been explored for machine-based intrusion detection. This manuscript section addresses various detection methods and related detection metrics.

S. Waskle et al. [1], in 2020 When wireless communications grow, the internet faces multiple security risks. The IDS helps to identify the device threats and the intruders can be identified. Various machine learning (ML) methods have previously been deployed on the IDS and have been used to improve performance on intruders identification and to improve IDS precision. The main component analysis (Principal component) and random forest classification methods were used in this paper to evaluate an effective IDS strategy. If the PCA leads to the organisation of the set of data by reducing the size of the data set and helps to differentiate the random forest. The findings obtained show that the methodology suggested functions more reliably in accordance with other approaches such as Support vector machine, Naïve Bayes and Decision Tree. The outcome obtained by the proposed approach is 3.24 minutes performance (min), 96.78 percent accuracy (percent), and 0.21 percent error (percent). With internet presence increasingly rapidly, the questions regarding security have also been noted. The solution suggested deals effectively with the identification of internet intruders. The proposed algorithm worked well, in comparison to previously used algorithms such as SVM, Naïve Bayes, and Decision Tree. With the proposed approach, it is possible to dramatically improve detection rates and false error rates. Here, the dataset is the data collection for knowledge exploration. The product of our method with the production time values (min) is 3.24 minutes, 96.78 percent of the accuracy rate (percent) and 0.21 percent of the error rate.

A. Ahmim et al. [2], in 2019 "This work provides a modern IDS architecture that integrates several approaches, like REP Tree, JRyp and Forest PA, focused on decision tree and rules-based concepts. In particular, the first and second methods take data set characteristics as the input and classify network traffic as the "Attack/Benign." This paper suggests a new intrusion mitigation model. The third classifier combines components from the initial data set in contrast to the outputs of the first and second classifiers. The test results obtained from the study of the proposed IDS utilising the CICIDS 2017 data collection indicate their superiority in terms of precision, detection rate, fabricated alert rate and overtime as compared to the latest existing devices. We have also placed out a hierarchical intrusion mitigation scheme focused on a mixture of the three different REP Tree, JRip and Forest PA classifiers. Two of them are operated in parallel and the third is fed. The evaluation of the 'CICIDS2017' data package showed that various well-known and modern machine learning models were outperformed by our hierarchical model, offering the highest TNR and the highest DR for 7 styles of assaults. Overall, 96,665 percent and a minimum FAR of 1,145 percent are the highest, with a maximum DR of 94,457 percent, but the slow computational period renders it ideal for IDS soft real-time systems.

M. Alrowaily et al. [3], in 2019 In terms of privacy security or data infringements, safety is the most critical question. In addition, criminals are releasing a new series of cyber attacks on the industry that block consumers from managing, networking or operating networks. That is why the growth of cyber-security studies, such as intrusion detection and prevention, is very significant. An successful method to malware attacks is the intrusion prevention system (IDS). A number of tests were conducted in this work using the intrusion detection dataset for seven algorithms for machine learning. Different efficacy measures were then used to assess the chosen algorithms. Experimental studies have shown that in terms of precision, memory, accuracy and F1-score, the K-Nearest Neighbors (KNN) classification is superior to other machine-learning classifications. Nevertheless, with the exception of KNN, both classifications studied their templates within a decent period of time. Several IDS experiments have been carried out to assess the effectiveness of seven computer classification classifiers, including AdaBoost, Random Woodland, NaiveBayes, Decision Tree, MLP, KNN and QDA. To detect intrusions, our knowledge array, which includes mild and most advanced popular attacks, was used (CICIDS2018). The test results indicate that the K-Nearest Neighbors (KNN) classification has a high quality in terms of diverse success indicators, such as precision, reminder, accuracy and F1 scores among others. However in an appropriate time frame the whole chosen machine learning classifiers with the exception of KNN learned their models.

Arif Yulianto et al. [4], This article discusses how through using Synthetic Minority Oversampling Technique (SMOTE), Principal Component Analysis (PCA), and Ensemble Feature Selection, the AdaBoost dependent Intrusion Detection System (IDS), centred on the newest and more challenging CIC IDS 2017 dataset, may improve its efficiency (EFS). It was proposed from previous research that the current dataset be handled using the AdaBoust classifier. However, owing to certain issues, such as a preparation gap and an inadequate set of classification techniques, the outcome is therefore weaker. In this analysis, SMOTE is chosen to solve the problem in order to create an approach to manage imbalance in training outcomes for efficiency changes in intrusion detection. Furthermore, to pick unique attributes for the latest dataset, key component analysis and set selection (EFS) are used. An extension of the functions is given for the latest dataset. Evaluation results show that under the AdaBoost Operational Characteristic Curve (AUROC) and the AdaBoost classifier with EFS and SMOTE, the proposed 92 percent AdaBoust classifier utilising PCA and SMOTE receives a precision, accuracy, retroactive and f1 value of 81.83 percent, 81.83 percent, 100 percent and 90.01 percent, respectively. The goal of the paper is to further enhance the efficacy of AdaBoost Intrusion Detection Systems based on the CIC IDS 2017 Dataset (IDS). The usage of the AdaBoost-based intrusion sensor (IDS) architecture in the recent and challenging CIC 2017 data set using the Synthetic Minority Surveillance Methodology, Principal Compound Analysis (PCA) and Ensemble Feature Selection Technique is addressed in this article (EFS). With a precision of 81.83 percent, a consistency of 81.83 percent, 100 percent and an F1 score of 90.01 percent, our suggested solution is considered to be beyond the efficiency of[6]. This is an irreplaceable aspect of the mechanism for data security. It is necessary to construct a high performance machine-learning IDS model because of the variety of system activities. In the future, we will use intrusion prevention approaches focused on machine learning for new and challenging databases, so that they can be utilised in real time.

D. Aksu et al. [5], in 2018 This study explored the performance metrics for helping vector machines and deep learning algorithms in the CICIDS2017 data set. The findings show that the deep learning algorithm has performed slightly better than the SVM. In the future, we will use the attempted port scan as well as other attack types focused on this data collection, with machine learning and data mining algorithms, apache hadoop and spark technologies. In contrast to the past, advancements in computer and networking technologies have made extensive and advanced changes. The usage of digital technologies provides tremendous benefits to individuals, companies and governments; nevertheless, they present certain difficulties. For instance, the security of important data, safety of storage data platforms, usability of knowledge, etc. Cyber crime, focused on these issues, is one of the most important subjects in today's world. By numerous groups such as criminal networks, technological workers and cyber activists, cyber violence has achieved a degree that can threaten public and national security, and this has led to many problems for individuals and organisations. Cyber terror Monitoring mechanisms for intrusion (IDS) were then established to combat cyber assaults. The purpose of this study was to classify port scan attempts utilising deep learning and vector machine (SVM) algorithms and 97.80 percent at 68.60 percent precision rates based on the new CICIDS2017 data collection.

H. Zhang et al. [6], in 2018 With the exponential development of Internet networks, network traffic data has become quite wide and complex, and the risk of interference has increased. With such high-speed traffic information, the IDS can not recognise intrusion behaviours. A real-time network IDS should be capable of handling vast volumes of network traffic data in order to identify suspicious traffic as easily as possible. We therefore suggest in this paper a network intrusion mitigation system based on a distributed random forest that can manage knowledge regarding high-speed transportation. There are three elements of this structure: a NetFlow-based data capture component, a pre-processing component of data and a classification-based intrusion detective component. In this post, we are using the random forest classification algorithm and applying it for real-time detection to the processing method distributed by Apache Spark. In order to check the reliability of the framework, we introduce the structure and run a set of comparative tests. The findings indicate that, in contrast with current solutions, the device provides adequate reliability and consistency and is thus suitable for the real-time monitoring of high-speed network interruption. A real-time detector framework is suggested for a high-speed network setting that will be introduced by the distributed RF detection concept based on Spark. The simulation phase of the whole device is applied by the data set for CICIDS2017 intrusion in a context consisting of logstash, kafka and the distributed Cluster Spark. First and foremost, softflowd exposes the PCAP file found in the CICIDS2017 data collection to model real network data traffic. The data is then transmitted to a Spark cluster with a distributed RF detection model through logstash and kafka. Experimental results and contrasts indicate that in real-time intrusion detection, there is shorter detection time in the proposed detection model, better precision, and in a high-speed network setting. We plan to implement new intrusion detection mechanisms in future work on the creation of a hybrid IDS to enhance the efficiency of device detection.

H. Azwar et al. [7], in 2018 Highly consistent wellness approach, emerging rates of protection hazards in the network commands. Researchers typically observed invasions in many different forms. In our article, we addressed the security phases of intrusion detection through the machine learning approach. The devolution of a powerful linking mechanism that effectively secures the device through a multiplicity of assaults has played a key role in this process. Intrusion detection (IDSs) A variety of techniques based on machine learning methods have been developed. However, in detecting all kinds of offences they are not successful. In our paper we have sponsored an exhaustive study of many machine learning methods to detect the origin of differences in perceiving intrusive behaviours linked to different techniques of machine learning. Often discussed are the drawbacks that surround each of them. Several machine learning data mining techniques were also used in the report. Compatible standard datasets exist severely to the asses and the identification mechanism is calculated. To estimate the efficacy of intrusion prevention techniques, such as DARPA98, KDD99, ISC2012, and ADFA13, etc, a number of databases are used, but we have also used the newest in our study. A great deal of accuracy has been given by CICIDS2017. For our own planned parameters, we have performed a major analysis of the existing datasets and have given an approximation outline for the IDS datasets. Through identifying concerns relevant to network-specific intrusion detection, we secure this right and provide a set of guidance principles for more research into anomaly detection. The output datasets for the IDS test and assessment were analysed in this article and a new framework was implemented to evaluate the data sets with: threats, confidentiality, open logs, complete capture, complete network setup, complete traffic, feature sets, heterogeneity, classified data and meta data (complete system configuration). The method proposed represents the approach of the organisation and the classification model. Matrix Expression of Uncertainty. The state of affairs is defined autonomously by a coefficient, W for each norm. We intend to develop and produce new data sets, which can be used to conform with any of the above requirements. The group in intrusion detection also faces challenging challenges, particularly after 20 lengthy periods of testing. A very uncertain problem remains the most successful way to identify obscure examples of attacks without unreasonable amount of false alarms, although some implications have recently exposed a potential tension in this area. The assessment and benchmarking of IDSs is also an imperative problem that if addressed will provide the hierarchical leaders and end customers with useful guidance. In addition, the use and implementation of IDSs would be improved by the assaults from IDS disruption alerts and inclusion. We believe that identification of disruption can become a standard and effective approach to ensure data framework. These concerns are discussed by various researchers and practitioners. This paper reviews numerous intrusion detection systems. Intrusion is identified in one way or another in all the approaches given here. In any case, criminals are prepared to discover new ways to breach defence protocols and methods. From the literature, it is clear that certain IDS operations rely on high time, memory and cost parameters that are isolated from focal points. Therefore, high accuracy, low false positive rate and low overhead overhead overhead must be available for every intrusion detection system. The precision of the strategies mentioned above is 92 per cent in our case.

M. Almseidin et al. [8], in 2017 The theory examines and measures the usefulness and performance of J48, Random Woodland, Random Tree, Judgement Table, Naive Bayes and Network. The following classifications will be addressed and evaluated. Tests and evaluations were used in this report. In all the tests, the KDD intrusion sensing dataset was included. In the KDD dataset, about 79 percent of DOS attacks, 19 percent of regular packets and 2 percent of other forms of attacks were in the basic form of attacks (R2l, U2R and PROBE). 148753 documents were obtained during the experiments as training data to create the training models for the selected machine classifiers. The research process is carried out on the basis of 60,000 random record instances. Several tests are measured (precision, false negatives, false positivity, truly negative and genuinen positivity).Experiments have shown that no machine-learning algorithm is available to manage these forms of attacks effectively. The decision table was the lowest false negative (0.002) value but was far from the highest precision identification. The decisions table was the most precise. On the other side, the Bayes network classifier is the highest value for the proper detection of daily packets. The lowest RMSE and false positive forest classifier rates recorded at the maximum level of accuracy 93.77 per cent. It seems like the random wood classification has sufficient performance parameters except for the inappropriate adverse parameter. Instead, all the elected classifiers, except the MLP, were authorised to develop their training models in an appropriate period. Moreover, true positive and mean accuracy scores alone are not necessary to identify the attack in order to ensure the network facilities are accessible and secretive. False negative and false positive frequencies must both be taken into consideration. The device of intrusion detection is one workaround for malicious attacks (IDS). Furthermore, perpetrators try to adjust their instruments and strategies. How ever will a negotiated IDS system not be followed. Multiple experiments have been carried out and tested in this article in separate machine learning classifications based on the KDD data collection. In order to evaluate the classifiers chosen, several performance measurements have been developed. The focus was placed on false negative and false positive performance tests in order to improve the detection rate of the intrusion detective unit. The experiments performed reveal the lowest value of false negatives in the random forest classification and the highest overall accuracy.

W. L Al-Yaseen et al. [9], in 2017 An integrated intrusion prevention device that identifies unknown threats in network traffic in real time presents an interesting obstacle. Computationally intensive, prove and uncertain risks in computing capital and time must be retrained for easily customised intrusion detection devices. This thesis suggests a framework named the Real- Time Multi-Agent Framework for an adaptive RTMAS-AIDS intrusion detecting system based on a multiple-agent system to adjust the intrusion detection system to unexpected attacks in real time. This methodology utilises hybrid SVM and ELM models for the identification of regular activity and recorded attacks. A adaptive SVM model is used to simultaneously perform and spread processes on MAS to detect and understand new attacks in real time. The results indicate that the proposed solution substantially lowered the training costs for unknown assaults, comparison with conventional methods. In addition, the successful KDDCup'99 data collecting reveals that RTMAS-AIDS can better identify samples, R2L attacks and U2R attacks than untrained hybrid SVM and ELM multi-level MUL hybrid SVM and ELM.RTMAS-AIDS detection efficiency, which is 95.86 percent. MAS-MLSE (MLSE and MLSE). RTMAS-AIDS, adaptive IDS, are prescribed in order to detect and to understand unknown assaults in real time. MAS builds an automatic infrastructure that speeds up data collection and makes it easier to retrain against unknown threats in real time. The two classification models of RTMAS-AIDS are the SVM and ELM multilateral models for typical behaviours, established attacks and an SVM adaptive model for acquiring and classifying unknown attacks. Instead of the large initial training datasets, tiny, high-quality training data sets generated by pre-treatment data were used to reduce the SVM and ELM training period. Data pre-processing often increases the performance of RTMAS-AIDS. RTMAS-AIDS has shown itself to be able to track unknown threats in real time and to understand in the experiment of KDDCup'99. Unknown assaults may also prevent injury. In comparison, the proposed system attained a total precision of 95.86% with an error alert rate of 2.13%. In all categories, particularly Sample and R2L attacks and U2R attacks were calculated superiors compared to MAS-MLSE and MLSE, the proposed method was superior. We plan to boost the reliability of RTMAS-AIDS in the future, as well as the processing time and new attacks with acceptable selection features, not only to pick up the amount of functions but also to increase system capacity.

Q. Niyaz et al. [10], in 2016 Network Intrusion Detection System (NIDS) supports network protection violations found by system managers in their organisations. But many challenges occur when a scalable, stable NIDS is generated in the event of sudden and unpredictable assaults. We propose a deep learning method for the development of such an effective, versatile NIDS. A profound form of education is used with the NSL-KDD benchmark dataset, self-teaching learning. Our contribution to a number of previous works is discussed and equated. The measurements are related to the consistency, precision, retrieval and f-measurement values we suggested to build a profoundly-learned and efficient NIDS approach. A sparse auto encoder and soft-max regression based on NIDS have been developed. We use the NSL intrusion data set - NSL-KDD to verify anomaly detection accuracy. We observed that NIDS was highly successful in checking outcomes for normal/anomaly identification in contrast to previously implemented NIDSs. Through adding strategies including the uncontrolled feature learning Stacked Car Encoder and the NB-Tree, the Random Tree or J48 for more classification, which would expand a sparse car encoder to a deepened believed network, the usefulness may be further improved. When applied directly to the data collection, the latter methods were found to be accurate. We will use profound learning technology in future to implement actual network NIDS in real-time. Another extremely influential research in this area may be on-the-go learning features in raw network headers rather than derived features.

C. O'Reilly et al. [11], in 2016 This analysis contains an IDS model that utilises Deep Learning – DMLP. The data set of CICIDS2017 contains data that can be used to test the model from real network traffic. The detection of malicious links that present significant challenges in the real network is a main concern for large data sets. The constant flow of data traffic is one critical problem that needs to be addressed fast. The processing of data may then be minimised without lowering precision and speed dependent on machine learning methods. In order to reduce the data set, the repetitive functions elimination method is used. The random tree structure of the forest is used as a disposal classifier. According to the test results the data collection is separated into two subgroups as malicious and normal communications queries. In the dataset of the classification method, meaning values for all attributes are still calculated. This lowers the data collection by 95%, depending on the four features, as opposed to the original size. The in-depth details – the DMLP model produces a smaller and more meaningful data collection with 89% accuracy. A large-scale traffic data collection in Hadoop and Spark ecosystems is anticipated to include an IDS in future work. This study suggests a malicious form of tracking (IDS) of computer networks. In 2017, CICIDS, the largest online dataset available, analyses the approach suggested. The aim is to analyse the impact on data storage of features and to discover which characteristics of the data are better distinguished so as to solve the challenges generated by Big Data. Therefore, persistent exclusion of features is defined by the random forest and the importance of the features is calculated. The structure of the Deep Multilayer Perceptron (DMLP) uses 91% reliable features to distinguish intrusions.

Y. M. Cheung et al. [12], in 2016 The detection of violence is called a pattern matching process. They proposed an abstract hierarchy based on hierarchical linkages of events definable as low audit trail events in order to identify intrusion signatures - i.e. attack trends. Intrusion signatures It helps to understand the complexity in this classification schema of detecting signatures at any step of hierarchy. It further determines the parameters for the broad range of intrusions that will follow patterns in all categories. Colored Petri nets with signature guides and vertices for system states to show signatures of risks. These patterns may be correlated to user-specific behaviour (e.g. vector assignments) and implemented only when the patterns are accurate. Petri automatic coloured networks are called the colourful Petri Network (CPA). CPA is a move from system states to intruded countries. The CPA shall also be related to pre- and post-conditions (e.g. conditions) and invariants that must be satisfied by corresponding series, before or after the game is played.

B. L. Santoso et al. [13], in 2016 Adopts two supervisory interference strategies focused on anomalies: multi-layer neural network and decision-making treaties (C4.5). Neural network offers a wide range of accuracy, but it was incredibly slow to identify new threats. In terms of generalisation accuracy and new assaults, decision-making trees displayed high efficiency. It has been used to retrieve the DARPA KDD dataset. This compilation of 24 forms of attacks can be classified in four major types: Denial of service (DOS), Remote User (R2L), and Root (U2R) and Scan. They also have used their methodologies on live network traffic in laboratories, including attacks which did not occur when DARPA was created. While the findings obtained are interesting in contrast with the previous ventures, such types of attacks also have poor detection rates. The study contributed two ways: to accept the principle of intrusion detection of irregularities during preparation and to incorporate a different class into new invasive instances (since these are unrepresented in the training dataset).

I. T. Jolliffe et al. [14], in 2016 Implementation of a technique which provides for the identification of attack type to identify network connections as regular or intrusive. A technique of dimension reduction was utilised in the detection of subcomponents that contain the most important information. The principal component analysis (PCA) was also known as Karhunen-Loève transform. The KDD dataset was used for evolving rules. In the first stage PCA limited the 41 features in the KDD data set to just three. The second step is to create a series of guidelines to identify actions as regular or abnormal using a genetic algorithm. Every law is an if-then formula for intrusion detection. The conditional component of the law consists of the AND function elements. This results in a test of the taxonomy of interference. The method provides in real time a high identification rate and a low fake-positive rate to pre-process network results. However, only three kinds of attacks were considered which were not enough to test the technique.

M. A. Ambusaidi et al. [15], in 2016 The use of the self-organizing Map and Adaptive Resonance theory 2 (ModifiedART2) to evaluate site logs and detect malicious and non-maliciously spectral visitors were analysed. Two unregulated learning algorithms were used. Three thousand-lion log records were recorded over a four-week period from web-based accesses to your domain. In order to indicate specific visitor sessions and build 10 features per session, they used pre-processing data before web visitors could be characterised. In a competitive learning process the SOM clustering approach uses several rounds to make the underlying algorithm respond in equal proportion to related input patterns. In tandem with the winner all rule the ART2 algorithm also utilises the principle of competitive learning, which ultimately produces various clustering outcomes. They describe four key categories of website users in their web log analysis: a human user, a decent crawler, a malicious crawler and an anonymous individual.

Z. Zhang et al. [29], In 2016 Create an IDS with the SVM Last Square algorithm integrated with the feature selection algorithm: Selection of Versatile Muy Knowledge (LS-SVM-IDS+FMIFS) functionality. The key idea is to delete redundant and unnecessary data features because these features slow down the classification process but also affect the quality of IDS classification. The assessment has shown that the algorithm for feature selection leads to features critical of LS-SVM-IDS for increased productivity and lower device costs. Shows the key stages of the identification frame: (1) data collections in which flows are collected for network packets, (2) data pre-processing in order to include pre-processing training and testing data, and the range of substantial features capable of effectively separating distinct groups, (3) classification training using the LS-SVM algorithm and (4) attack recapture; The model was studied using KDD, NSL-KDD and Kyoto 2006+ 3Datasets. The NSL-KDD dataset has been incorporated in the original KDD dataset to answer those problems. Intrusion detection via computer networks has achieved promising achievements by the established IDS. LSSVM-IDS + FMIFS are usually more powerful relative to the other cutting-edge algorithms.

M. Toulouse et al. [16], in 2015 Used algorithms for machine learning to create models that infer regular network traffic from malicious network traffic. A mechanism for data reduction to eliminate irrelevant and redundant functionality (ie, collection of functions) leads to a reduction in the process time in its proposed architecture. They were used with four separate functional selection approaches to test three classification models (5 closest neighbour, C4.5 decision tree and Naïve Bays). For training and model checking the Kyoto 2006+ data collection is used. Although selection of the function decreases the number of characteristics, the effects of classification have shown that it preserves or does not dramatically reduce results. They conclude that feature selection is an important pre-processing phase in the IDS application domain and should not be taken lightly.

O. Kilinc et al. [17], in 2015 IDS recommended that a huge volume of data and a high-speed world be dealt with (i.e. Internet and network services). The 4 layered IDS framework includes the capture, filtration and load balance layer, parallel processing layer (e.g. hadoop) and decision-making layer. this system is proposed (see Figure 2.3). The test was performed with the DARPA, KDD and NSL-KDD. In comparison, the number of input features from 41 to 9 is lowered with two feature selection approaches and traffic analysis by DARPA. At first a high-speed capture system captures the flow of network packets. The second layer uses the In-Memory intruders database to scan and compare the incoming traffic efficiently to identify it as a regular flux or intrusion. Then, the unspecified flow traffic with data on the packet header to the third tier of master servers is completed (i.e. Hadoop). It also compensates for the strain by deciding the packets to which master server dependent on IP adresses is sent. Hadoop has a MapReduce code that uses the map and reduce function, which includes certain calculation code parameters to determine the values of nine variables. The overall performance is improved as MapReduce runs concurrently. Finally, the characteristic values are passed on to the decision maker who classifies the flows as benevolent or threats, based on the values of their features. Five ML algorithms, namely J48, REP-Tree, the forest random tree, conjunctive law, SVM and Naives Bay, were used for this layer. In terms of processing time and precision, both REPTree and J48 achieved the best efficiency.

O. Kilinc et al. [18], in 2015 The usage for Classification & Regression Trees (CART) IDS algorithms and Bayesian Networks (BN) was researched. These two paradigms were used as hybrid classifications and group classifications. DARPA, from which a subset was picked randomly, was the data source used in this analysis. The range of features was also made for measurement time. Next, BN and CART with complete and subset functionality were tested separately. The 41-characteristics score was compared with a range of 17 by BN and 12 by CART. With a smaller collection of functions, BN fared worse than with the standard class. CART reached 100% natural classification accuracy with decreased data set and improved U2Rand R2L accuracy. A reduced collection of features (i.e. 12 and 17) and 41 of the dataset were used to validate the ensemble model and the workflow in Figure 2.4a is shown. The final decisions were made as follows in the ensemble method: the output of each paradigm is weighted accordingly. The final outcome is selected correctly, until the two paradigms agree. If the judgement of the paradigm clashes, so the one of the highest weight is preferred. On the basis of the findings, the ensemble models have concluded that they work more successfully than the two person paradigms. After summarising the output models, they built a hybrid IDS architecture for both ensemble and individual classifiers. Finally, the hybrid model was used to more reliably diagnose standard, probe or DOS instances.

L. Dhanabal et al. [19], in 2015 Proposed an IDS hybrid multi-level classifier. This method merged an unattended learner and a supervised learner (i.e. Bayean clustering) (i.e. Decision tree C4.5). In this job, the KDD dataset was used. The C 4.5 model classified instances in three groups DoS, Study and Other in the first stage of the grouping. At this point, U2R and R2L attacks as well as benevolent instances are listed as others. Step 2 used Bayesians as attacks and benevolent instances to distinguish others in (U2Rand R2L) using just 4 of the 41 functions. These features have been selected by applying a series of metrics such as the information gain, after determining the value of each feature. In stage 3, the models C4.5 were used only with 14 functions to distinguish U2R and R2L. This move is much easier to perform provided the isolation of the Benevolent instances at stage 2. C4.5 is eventually used to separate into its variants more classes in each attack type. The experimental result showed a highly efficient detection rate with a very small false-negative rate while, contrasting with other common methods, retaining a fair false-alarm frequency. Unknown attacks that lack the training data set are nevertheless very poor.

M. O. Ulfarsson [20], in 2015 Proposed a set of three foundation classifiers (Decision Trees (DT), Support Vector Structures (SVM), and the DT and the SVM hybrid sys-tem). Using KDD as the training dataset to construct the IDS model. Each model included additional detail on the behaviours detected (i.e. five distinct classes) to be classified in this experiment. The final product of the ensemble classification is determined by the maximum score of the base models. Each model's score is calculated by allocated weights that reflect the individual output prediction on the training data set. For this purpose, the ensemble classifier can use a model score if a particular example can be classified and if all models offer different opinions. The top score model is known as the winner and used to determine the final result. Obviously, the ensemble approach uses the misclassification disparities and increases overall efficiency.

E. Vasilomanolakis et al. [21], in 2015 Proposed the fusion of three classifiers to detect a single class for a heterogeneous ensemble. Linear Genetic Programming (LGP), Random Forest (RF), and Adaptive Euro-Fuzzy Inference Method (ANFIS) were used in the development of network-based IDS. They followed the following algorithms. During the preparation, the same data sets were used for every algorithm, i.e., LGP, ANFIS and RF. The KDD dataset was used in this analysis. In the extraction of essential features, Rough Set technique and Discrete Particle Swarm Optimization (RST-BPSO) were used. The initial 41 features for all grades have been narrowed to 15 and for each class there are different features. The machine then employed the weighted voting process, after construction of base classifiers, to decide the final classification. Overall, relative to the two other algorithms, the efficiency of LGP is higher, while ANFIS and RF are practically the same. It has been shown that the ensemble method is greater than the strongest classifier alone.

R. Raphael et al. [22], in 2014 It was analysed how three paradigms are implemented to increase the performance of IDSs according to the network. They also used bagging, boosting and piling systems to resolve intrusion sensing problems in a manner that increases precision and reduces false positive frequency. The four data mining algorithmes used as basic learners for this group were naïve Bayes, J48, JRip, and iBK (nearest neighbor). The NSL-KDD dataset has been included. J48 has done better than the other 3 methods with respect to the four baseline classifiers used in terms of the best accuracy, the lowest false positive probability, and faster execution time. You suggested that the approaches used in the identification of current attacks were quite successful; nevertheless, new attacks were successfully detected. The usage of bagging, boosting and piling did not change dramatically. Stacking was the only paradigm that led to a significant reduction in false positive rates. They then concluded that the topic of intrusion detection is unqualified for a good solution. How ever, with recent advances in machine power, this problem may be resolved rapidly. In addition, it is also necessary that errors except in a small way are minimised in the region of IDS.

D. J. Weller et al. [23], in 2014 Proposed the use of an ensemble concept to detect new web Server threats using an anomaly-based Intrusion Detection System. The log boosting algorithm, along with the RF algorithm, is a stacking technique because of its strength when dealing with noise and outliers. It was tested using only HTTP traffic using 2 datasets (NSL-KDD and UNSW-NB15). As a pre-processing stage, a hybrid function selection technique was used to pick only significant functions, which reduces the overall detection time. The number of features in NSL-KDD has been decreased from 41 to 10, with the numbers decreased from 43 to five for UNSW-NB15. the anomaly detection ensemble model suggested workflow. workflow The authors ensured that there were entirely separate attack traffic in each training and test area. The log it improves the classification algorithm has achieved excellent overall accuracy and also a low false alarm rate. The findings have however shown that the detection rate for such unexplored attacks in both datasets was very poor.

2.2 Summary

Literature analyses are elementally discussed in this chapter in most cases based on previous books. There broadly is also debate on classification of intrusion detection systems, types of indeed protected systems, ids for all intents and purposes data management technology, basically dataset assessment, and feature collection. There fairly were also reflections about the benefits and weaknesses of prior works.

CHAPTER THREE

Problem Identification

3.1 Identification of Problem

Misrepresentation of data is clearly a huge challenge in the network, and even though it has to deal with massive dataset, it gets rather repetitive. The bigger the initiative, the problem of deficiency detection is made more complex by an automated measuring and measurement process and the expense of the mission is increased. The Internet has demonstrated the need to ensure the protection of confidential and real-time data flowing across networks because of fast-growing network communications technologies. Several cryptographical methods are known to construct the big data security system, but these cryptography methods will soon be broken down due to an improvement in hacker calculation ability. The evolution of IDS models has contributed to several difficult problems. The identification and detection of misuse abnormalities are both impaired by these problems:

- **Data in large dimensions (Feature Selection)**

To be able to evaluate the irregular behaviour of normal behaviour, a significant number of computer network data must be gathered. The network data collected are identified with several attributes, including protocol sort, link length, port destination, source port, etc. Thus the wide size of these attributes makes the IDS method with higher error rates more complex and complicated. Some features are irrelevant and repetitive to attack patterns, and the identifying method can slow down. For the performance of the adopted detection techniques, the use of feature selection or feature extraction is therefore required.

- **Time to forecast and correctly**

By handling their capital and transactions across the network, businesses from various places earn profit. Malware safety, access control, firewalls, email security, IPS and similar concepts and devices actually lack 100%

security of the data and network-hosted services. Since data values are of little benefit if data protection and privacy are jeopardised, the big data security is still a major problem for any solution. One of the key securities problems of real-time data is the monitoring and avoidance of network intrusions that are not predictive because the network is the backbone of big data. The confidentiality, integrity and availability of big data resources and services can impact these intrusions.

- **Identification of unknown intruders**

In several computer networking networks cybercrimes occurred seriously and constantly since the intruders continue to create a new type of intruders. The unidentified malicious attacks emerged from the needs of the information infrastructure for free use and sharing. Computer networks now need big open systems for sharing.

- **Classification of complexity and insecurity**

Various forms of IDS analysis have concentrated on addressing the uncertainty of traffic data and have to be able to understand and treat ambiguously. In other words, the relation to an intruder class or regular class is to any extent too vague. Certain types of intruders, often integrated into the packets and impossible to distinguish from usual connections, are difficult to recognise entirely. The concern may be that the patterns of these intruders are identical to those of regular connections, or that the distinction between normal and intruders is complex.

3.2 Aims of study

In this analysis and, therefore, a thesis have been created, some main research objectives have been identified in light of the criteria for an effective IDS and its optimum reliable market as well as functionality. The goals of this research are to ensure effective IDS. In general, the research goals were divided into two categories: general goals and particular goals. The general goals are certain targets which are suggested or planned to attain as definitive or final objectives, while on the other hand particular objectives are directed at achieving ultimate general objectives through the application of some robust strategies and relevant technologies. The basic targets are the technological requirements that should be applied for the proposed research model to achieve the overall research objective. The following are granted both general and particular objectives:

3.2.1 General goals:

The aim of this analysis is to establish a network-based anomaly scheme that helps to identify network traffic anomalies. The data mining algorithm can be used. This system is characterised by high speed network traffic processing and analysis, by decreasing the FA (False Alarm) rate to a minimum, by identifying the infusion in real time and by using the known attack pattern during the training stage to improve the identification rate. The system detects new intruders correctly.

3.2.2 Specific Goals:

- To provide a description of the big knowledge and the associated work in the field of safety analysis.
- Investigate various strategies used to adapt intrusion detection over standard files.
- To build intrusion and multiple intruders models to protect the Big Data environment.
- Validation of the models proposed and evaluation of the model results.
- Checking the feasibility of the approaches proposed relative to current ones
- For future studies to conclude and propose.

CHAPTER FOUR

Methodology

4.1 Introduction

4.1 Introduction

This work can help you understand how auto-encoders (AE) and (PCA) concept interpretation can be used efficiently. The researchers used CICIDS 2017 intrusion detection and prevention data collection, [4] which comprises isolated data files, to replicate the reduction of the dimension of features as proof of concept and for validating accuracy. Per file represents a specific form of network traffic and attacks and how long they have been identified. The data collected were collected by a total of five days from Monday to Friday according to data set measurements. Internet traffic sends out every 10 seconds small sections of the results, each with different features. The sum of successful traffic happens on Monday, although there are further attacks on Wednesday, Thursday and Friday. As we have consolidated and fed all our documentation into AE and PCA units, a smaller dataset has been developed, which allows it simpler to draw conclusions and draw some of our results. The basic concept of the proposed system is presented in Figure 1.

4.2 Dataset of CICIDS2017

4.2 Dataset of CICIDS2017

The details given in CICIDS2017 contain realistic transit traffic that represents network operation in the actual abstract actions of a total of 25 individuals. In the user's profile, basic protocols including HTTP, HTTPS, FTP, SSH and the email protocol were found. In order to provide awareness of the network traffic events in a set of certain functions, such as those described above the developers focusing on statistic metrics like minimum, mean and standard deviation.

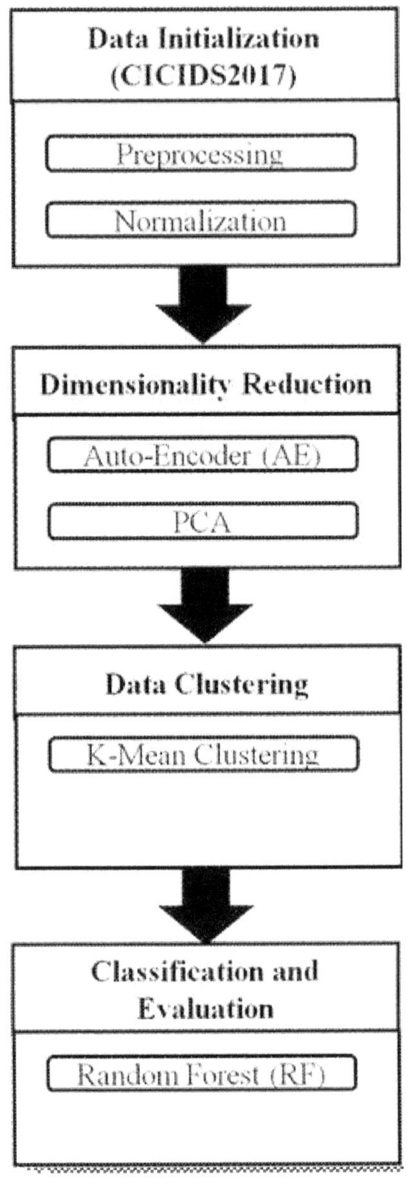

Figure 4.1 Methodology

i. The packet size distribution is distinct.
ii. The number of flow rate packets.
iii. The extra sum you earned.
iv. Distributions of the moment the protocols are sent.
v. There are also consistencies or trends in this contrast.

CICIDS2017 looks at multiple scenarios of attacks representing traditional family attacks. This may involve a Brute Force Assault, Heart Bleed Attack, a Botnet, a DoS, a DDoS, a Network Attack and an Intrusion Attack.

The dataset is available in two formats by the developers:

1. The computers catch all of the complete packets in the packet capture format.
2. First, there is a broad data collection to play with. Second, the datasets support with computer learning purposes.

Internet and Security Cognitive Defeitnancy was assessed by analysing existing abnormal packets in network traffic. For data processing, the total amount of documents is 2.3 billion. The observed benevolent files are approximately two million three thousand three hundred eighty thousand reports (83.3% of the data), while the harmful files are approximately four hundred forty thousand reports (83.3% of the data) (16.7 percent of the data). One of the specific sources that holds the most current attack details is CICIDS2017. Anything save for the CICIDS2017 was selected as the most comprehensive IDS benchmark challenging the latest concepts presented. Table 2 offers a comprehensive description of the different threats, with a review of the basic danger attributes, as well as the attack's geography and location. CICIDS2017 is a free label dataset with a total of 2721,043 records, 78 features, and a single description for the effects of the network type. A little bit of pre-calculated average, peak, min, stddev, and a lot of data details is available.

The data has been carefully sorted. Influenza epidemics are currently very difficult to model in IDS because influenza has two circulating strains, and these imbalanced datasets give rise to a large number of false positives and false negatives. The model in question is an attempt to detect false positives without over fitting, and allow more false positives than false positives.

4.2.1 Data Preprocessing

A preprocessing capability is applied to the CICIDS2017 dataset in this study by transforming the IP (Internet Protocol) address to the an integer representation. We learn the source IP and the target IP address while we have the normal resource locator for the packet (Dst IP). These two are transformed into a number that represents the equivalence of their integer values. This study is updated to split the details into a training set and a test set with an 80:20 ratio.

Step for preprocessing:

- First, we will remove all the pre-calculated mean, variance, std, min and max values
- For a smaller feature space.
- Then proceed to encode the categorical labels.
- Drop all missing values.
- Finding missing values
- Find all infinite or infinite values
- Drop all nan values and remaining non-finite values
- Make sure the data frame is clean

Table 4.1 : Feature count before and after pre-processing

Pre-processing	Entries	Features
Before	2830743	79
After	2827876	45

4.2.2 Normalization

We can re-scale the data in the next step such that the characteristics have a range of values that does not fall too far from the nominal value of the function. Many of the attributes used in the initial dataset are distinct from [0, 1]. Some of the characteristics used in the initial dataset differ between [0, ??]. In order to restrict the range of values between 0 and 1, the same attribute is generalised for humans, which is then interpreted by the auto-encoder for practical reduction.

$$x_i = \frac{x_i - x_{min}}{x_{max} - x_{min}}$$

The value of a certain function of an input is calculated like this. In this example, xmin is the lowest, and xmax is the limit.

4.3 Features High dimensional Reduction

4.3 Features High dimensional Reduction

A variety of approaches ranging from dimensionality reduction methods to data reduction strategies have been used by computer scientists for numerous purposes, such as minimising the overhead of numerical computation, reducing noise in the data, and correctly imaging the details. The use of the Missing Value Ratio (MVR) process is another way to reduce the dimensionality of details. A more efficient way to work when dealing with missing values is the Minimum Variance Ray (MVR). There is virtually no missing data for the serum levels of the ingredient for all CICIDS2017 events. Consequently, the Missing Meaning Ratio method was not involved in our research. Like the Forward Function Construction ("FFC") and the Backward Feature Removal ("BFE") methods, there are also other electronic paraphrasing approaches. High-dimensional datasets, such as the CICIDS2016, need very long periods of computation and are not adequate for BFE and FFC. We did not discuss these approaches as a result of this. The PCs are calculated quite easily in the PCA technique, for very big datasets, and can be used for a wide variety of problems; their usage is quite general, sometimes used as a "dimensionality reduction." The process of reducing dimensionality of auto-encoder and deep learning takes a dataset and determines one of its many, many dimensions to edit from the training data to render the auto-encoder difficulty. It uses AE (supervised) and PCA (unsupervised) attribute reductions for the reduction of functions. In terms of dimensionality reduction, one of the main fundamental discrepancies between AE and PCA is that there is no assumption of linearity in the outcomes of the auto-encoder strategy. As its name implies, under the given reconstruction error metric, the auto encoder optimizer works out the function via the weights that best encode the details. And it is definitely true, at least in terms of the degree to which the diminished data is obtained. [35].

4.3.1 Auto-Encoder (AE) Based Dimensionality Reduction

This section introduces the sparse Auto-Encoder learning algorithm[38], one way to train feature reduction automatically in unattended environments. The design of the auto-encoder that was generated can be seen in figure 2. The first dimensions are reduced to a secret description that contains of one or even more hidden layers s a= in the input vector x= (x1,x2,...,xn) . The (a1,a2,...,am). Let j be the neuron counter parameter in the current layer, let j be the neuron counter parameter in the previous layer, and let k be the k-th neuron in the previous layer. With the following formula, the difference in production for the neuron in the hidden layer may be defined.

$$a_j^{(l)} = f(z_j^{(l)}) = f(\sum_{i=1}^{n} W_{ji}^{(l-1)} . a_i^{(l-1)} + b_j^{(l-1)})$$

The weight matrix of the secret layer is defined in this network by W µRm tunn and the weight bias is µRm. The feature vector is one parabolic, f(z) =1/(1+exp(-z)) is one parabolic function for −z <z>1. To optimise the model parameters, I allocate W and B at random as each back spread phase, I start with a random b and choose W at random.

$$J(W, b; \hat{x}, x) = \frac{1}{k} \sum_{i=1}^{k} (\frac{1}{2} ||\hat{x} - x||^2) + \frac{1}{\lambda} \sum_{l=1}^{l_s - 1} \sum_{j=1}^{m} \sum_{i=1}^{n} (W_{ji}^{(l)})^2$$

Parameter λ is selected to monitor the regularisation time of all weights

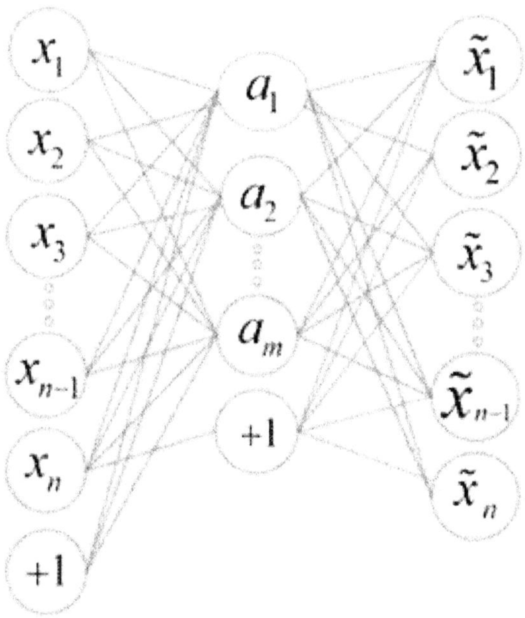

Figure 4.2. The design of an Auto Encoder.

a specific layer, and the last number indicates the overall number of layers. To ensure that the train has further situations where there is a finite supply of products, the loss function is iteratively optimised. At each iteration, the loss function penalises the KL divergence between a Bernoulli random variable with mean ρ and the optimal value of $\hat{\rho}_j$.

$$\hat{\rho}_j = \frac{1}{k}\sum_{i=1}^{k}\left[a_j^{(i)}(x^{(i)})\right]$$

Where a(i) and in auto-encoder denotes the triggering of secret unit j, and k is the sample of the training.

$$J_{sparse}(W,b) = J(W,b;\hat{x},x) + \beta \sum_{j=1}^{m} KL(\rho \,||\, \hat{\rho}_j)$$

This sparsity is guaranteed to have the consequence of allowing the hidden layer to be close to the hidden layer, as it means that sparse activations are collected from the training data for each unit in the hidden layer. To control the weight for the representation of the scarcity penalty, the value of β and the value of γ are selected. Computed, when expanded to a single hidden layer and a dimension of n, the computation necessary to operate the configuration of the auto encoders is focused on the reduction values of R and ε (0,1)

$$O(n.\,(R \times n) + (R \times n)\,.n) = O(Rn^2 + Rn^2) = O(n^2)$$

In this analysis, a sparse auto-encoder with two secret layers is used. The roles of sigmoid activation are selected, but the weights are separately trained. There are 81 neurons in each of the 81 input layers in the My-QIK-Fusion input network, allowing for the number of 816 features in the data set for CICIDS2017. The sparse auto-first encoder's secret layer was able to effectively reduce the measurements to 70 characteristics with a good approximation of error. From 1024 to 64, all the functions that were in the second hidden layer were reduced. The resulting sparse auto-encoder may be conditioned to work in the very last step where the weights are modified to the learning phase. Set the parameter values for this algorithm to 0.0008, with a decrease in weight of λ= 0.0008. In order to prevent the objects from becoming too large, mathematicians change the weight of each piece. The amount of the sparsity penalty shall be 5 and the term of the penalty shall be 6. The penalties for sparsity and sparse parameters are meant to disrupt the secret units, prohibiting the characteristics from becoming heavily reliant on each other. The algorithm is found in Table 3.1, and Table 3.2 still illustrates the design concepts.

4.3.2 Principle Component Analysis (PCA) Based Dimensionality Reduction

The Key Factor Analysis is the approach used to decrease the dimensionality of the specified dataset, more specifically. The study of the key components is one of the most powerful and effective methods to minimising data measurements and produces the required results[6]. The key elements are used in this data reduction strategy, one of which allows the provided material to construct a smaller set of unique items such as attributes. As a dataset, this method takes all the input, and is made up of a very high amount of attributes, since the data set dimension is very high. Because these two data sets are on the same data set axis, they should be looked at in such a manner that the size of the initial data set can be reduced. When the first key components have been determined, the correlation matrix reveals the scatter of the points with a somewhat smaller difference between the rows and columns. It is necessary to conduct the primary care battery test in the following manner:

1. All the d variables are independent and non-negative in the specified dataset.
2. The mean vector calculation is carried out on an ESM for each dimension.
3. For the whole collection of results, measure the covariance matrix.
4. Multiply the proprietary value with the proprietary vector (e1, e2, e3... 'ed) that gives the most proprietary value (v1, v2, v3,vd).

5. Use the formula to sort each of the eigen values in descending order and select the number of vectors with the highest value of n as their own value.
6. A new sample space is generated by the usage of this M-form.
7. The samples offer the best risk of defining the patient's genotype.

This portion would be applied using the Principal Component Analysis (PCA) approach. The purpose of the PCA is to minimise the set of categorical data inputs. PCA (Principal Component Analysis) discovers a data transition that eliminates the data's dimensionality while accounting for almost all the variance. One of the first multivariate regression methods is PC analysis. The fundamental theory of the PCA is focused on the projection-based process. Here, the original XεRn dataset of n columns (features) is projected onto the XεRK representation subspace of k or less dimensions (fewer columns), thus retaining the nature of the original Xε dataset. The algorithm you can think about is as follows:

Algorithm 3.1: The new Auto-Encoder pseudo-code.

Dimensionality Reduction Using AE

Training:

1. In a batch method, execute the feed forward transfer on all the training instances and compute the average output.

   a(1), and a. (2)
2. Take the mean of the vector, and then calculate the output, sparsity mean, and the error of the cost function.

   J(w, b; x, x^).
3. Compute the cost function seeing that the autoencoder is sparse.

   JSparse (W,b)
4. In the hippocampus, backpropagating the error to update the weights and biases for all the layers.

Dimensionality Reduction:

Compute the reduced features from the hidden layer.

Table 4.2: Design Principles

Parameters	**Value**	**Description**
λ	0.0008	Weight decay
B	6	Sparsity penalty
ρ	0.005	Sparsity parameter

When a data set is N-dimensional, it is reorganised into K-dimensional data sets using the preprocessing stage and a clustering approach is used for more succinct data sets. In the preprocessing method, (steps 1 through 4 below) the data is normalised to a mean of zero and a variance of one. The second phase (step 5 to 8) of the process was where the CovM (covariance matrix) is measured, the matrix are calculated to be the eigenvectors and eigenvalues.

1. Also combined and normalised to its mean and variance, where a sum of all individual values offset to one total, and by its mean and variance of all instances in the dataset, can be compared.

$$\mu = \frac{1}{m}\sum_{i=1}^{m} X_{(i)}$$

1. Replace X(i) with X(i)−μ, .
2. Rescale the domain of measures to have unit variance.

$$\sigma_j^2 = \frac{1}{m}\sum_{i} (X_{j(i)})^2$$

1. Substitute Xj(i) with Xj(i)/σ for both of them.
2. The Covariance Matrix CovMas calculation is as follows:

$$Cov_M = \frac{1}{m}\sum (X_{(i)})(X_{(i)})^T$$

6. Measure CovM's Eigen-vectors and their related Eigen-values.
7. Sort Eigen-vectors and choose k Eigen-vectors with the maximum Eigen-values to form W by reducing Eigen-values.

8. Use W to transform the samples into a new subspace by using Equation (3.9).

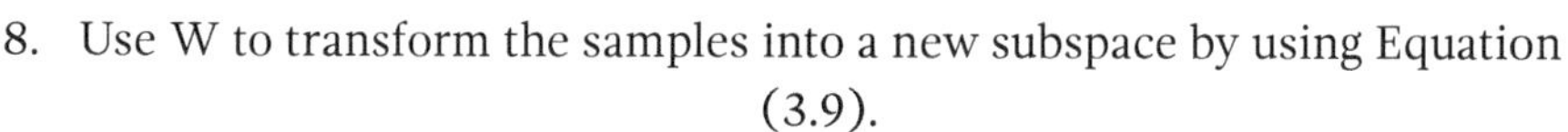

y=WT: y=WT......................................4.10

When X is an ad-1 dimensional vector that describes one sample, the transformed k-1 dimensional sample is y in the current subspace. The computational cost of the built-in PCA execution is based on the number of features P of each data point[64].The PCA reduction ratio (RR) can be defined as the ratio of goal numbers to original dimensions. The lower the RR amount, the higher the PCA.

4.4 Clustering of data

4.4 Clustering of data

Cluster-analysis or clustering is the method of assigning entity sets to groups (referred to as clusters), so that items of the same class are more connected to each other (somehow or other) than those of other clusters. For a wide variety of real-time applications grappling with massive quantities of data, data mining classification and clustering techniques are beneficial. Any of the applications of data mining include text classification, targeted publicity, medical research, and intrusion detection systems. Intrusion detection in knowledge security is an act in which acts to threaten the confidentiality, integrity or availability of a property are detected. Intrusion detection systems are automated systems for the recognition of anomalies from the system's normal conduct and use. They detect attacks using the grouping and clustering algorithms in data mining techniques. Most of the new approaches rely on anomaly detection systems becoming more generalised and having a broader spectrum relative to harassment detection systems. For both anomaly and abuse identification, data mining techniques may be applied. It is possible to use clustering techniques to create clusters of data samples corresponding to the system's usual use. In contrast to classification-based approaches, clustering-based methods may detect new threats.

4.4.1. K-means Clustering Algorithm

The computer makes clusters by calculating the distance of points and then classifying objects (invasions) to the cluster. Unlike grouping, learning is unattended and there is not sufficient knowledge for the labels of the learning data that was used to fill the model with. However, for anomalous identification, the safest approach is by building a model on the pattern of the phenomenon. When gathering data about a phenomenon, the essential job is to be able to measure the distance or resemblance that occurs between the observations. For affinity calculation, what is needed is that the fingerprint be attuned to the limit or to the shortest range, so that it is possible to decide whether there is some error or abnormality. However, some different implementations are focused on the Euclidean distance and in the Euclidean dimensions are approximately two vectors X and Y of the distance. The euclidean distance can also be described using the Pythagorean theorem as the square root of the total variance of the same vector dimensions. Finally, all clustering and classification algorithms had to be channelled appropriately, primarily to handle the aggregate network data and the other variables.

Here I am dividing data segments into groups dependent on connection trends using the K-means algorithm. One of the many algorithms of clustering is the K-means that both computers use. K-means group the data according to their characteristics and create own classes for a certain number of K clusters. Related feature values are found in data clustered into the same package. A positive integer must be supplied in advance to account for the number of clusters. The calculations in a K-means algorithm are as follows.

1. The eight points given (indices, months and days) are used to construct a form of data that is clustered into clusters. These points show the primary category (e.g., red circle).
2. In certain instances, data is assigned to the group closest to the centroid.
3. Once all of the details have been assigned, the positions of all the centroids are recalculated.
4. Step (3) & (2) with a 5-step process before unchanged of the centroid.

This mechanism allows the cancer to be split into cell classes. K-means uses a K meaning similar to 5 in the preprocessing results, so clusters are quick to identify. While all of our data is in the file, we have a dataset which contains all 4 attack types, including DoS, Sample, U2R and R2L.

Clustering K-means is one of the simplest clustering algorithms to do. This algorithm brings the number of clusters, 'k' and calculates the dataset's 'k'-cluster partition. The clustering is performed to render the intra-cluster similarity ("sum of squared differences") is large and the inter-cluster similarity is tiny. All the way 'K' is a positive integer number given in advance. K reflects a better reliable of grouping in an ordered and standardised fashion than hierarchical clustering and yields better performance. Through analysing the test data , is grouped into 5 forms of the datasets, namely, the attack content dataset assaulting content dataset with interference, Welcome dataset regular dataset, Aggressive dataset offensive dataset, and hello world dataset. There are these steps to the process that sorts the data:

1) Define the number of K clusters.
2) Initialize the centres of the K cluster. This can be achieved by randomly splitting all objects into K clusters, calculating their centroids, and ensuring that all centroids are distinct from each other. Alternatively, the centroids may be initialised to the selected K, separate objects.
3) Eradicate all artefacts and measure the distances of all clusters to the centroids. Assign each object to the cluster of the closest centroid.
4) Recalculate the centroids of the two modified clusters.
5) Repeat step 3 until the centroids no longer shift.

A distance function is necessary to measure the distance (i.e. similarity) between two objects. The most widely used distance function is the Euclidean function:

$$d(x, y) = \sqrt{\sum (x_i - y_i)^2} \quad \text{..................................4.11}$$

Where $x = (x_1..x_m)$ and $y = (y_1...y_m)$ are input data vectors having the characteristics of quantitative m. Both characteristics relate similarly to the importance of the function within the Euclidean distance function. However, when various characteristics are typically measured with different measurements or with different sizes, before the distance function is implemented, they have to be standardised.

4.5. Classification

4.5. Classification

We have various kinds of classifiers, ranging from astronomy to biology, including physics, and also business systems, which have been created and used for different forms of applications. - of these algorithms has its own specific characteristics, although a related definition can arise from some algorithms. It is the method of selecting a certain form of classifier model that may influence the outcome of precision, the time it takes to create the model, and the rate of detection.

4.5.1 Random Forest Algorithm

One of the most common methods or approaches that scientists and researchers use in data science is Random Forest. Via supervision in individual instances, it distinguishes groups. It is called "forest of randomness," which implies that the game would aim to build a forest to make it random. There is a clear connection between the amount of trees in the forest and the type of valuable outcomes or knowledge it may produce: the more trees, the more useful the outcomes are among large quantities of trees. One thing you have to be cautious of is that it is not the same thing as what I did in the past of China to create the forest and collect knowledge about the forest.

Random Forests encourages many to cultivate trees for classification. In a certain way, every tree is grown:.

(1) Where N, sample N cases at random, but replacing, is used from the original data for the number of cases in the training collection. This specimen is the training collection for the tree.

(2) If there are M input variables available, m is defined such that m variables are picked at random from M and the best split is selected from this m to split the network at each node. The value of m stays constant throughout forestry growth.

(3) Every tree is grown to the greatest degree practicable. There will be no pruning open.The Random Forest algorithm has many great advantages. Some of the advantages are:

- Accuracy.
- Runs efficiently on large amounts of information.
- We handle thousands of data points with no data loss.
- Provides effective methods for estimating data to be missing
- Is ideal when large numbers of variables are missing.

4.6 Tools and Environment

4.6 Tools and Environment

4.6.1 Anaconda

Anaconda is a distribution of python and R that brings data science through the 21st century and machine learning. The conditions of the licence are entirely free and open source, with more than 1400 separate bundles. Anaconda, as the main wrapper, requires entry to all libraries and also offers a focal point for libraries that may involve science computation. From the terminal, you would be able to instal a library.

4.6.2 Jupiter Notebook

The Jupiter notebook is an area in which calculations may be done on a user's computer within the browser. The Jupyter notebook is simply a JSON document that contains an organised list of I/O cells and can contain code, mathematics, text, graphs/plots, and other content forms. The Jupyter notebook encourages the author to function in the browser for code without needing to run the whole project again even when they wish to play with just a limited portion of the code. There is the opportunity for this device to have a lot of functionality.

4.6.3 Scikit-learns to learn

Inside the Python programming language, Scikit-learn is a library to help do mathematical numerical computation. In order to cope with regression, sorting and clustering, the framework has various functionality.

4.6.4 NumPy

Numpy provides a python library which provides support for large multi-dimensional arrays and matrices to be constructed and modified. Electronic cigarette (e-cigarette) contains sequences for operating on arrays of high level mathematical functions. Matplotlib is a library for visualisation that also encourages computational mathematics. A graphical annotation surface enables various kinds of graphic display of findings to be plotted.

4.6.5 Pandas

Python is another programming language for general purposes, it also has a function for data analysis and comprehension. Pandas are a sort of frame for details. Pandas are so smart that, especially in the suburbs, they can be used for a variety of different purposes. There are numerous applications for this procedure, including data cleaning. Around 80% of the amount of time spent on a machine learning initiative is spent on data cleaning, according to IBM analytics. Broad datasets accessible in good places are often missing, limiting a model's usefulness. The .isnull() function is defined for this as an illustration to show that not all insights or mistakes are inevitable.

4.6.6 The Design of the Device

This thesis was carried out on a device that has the following configuration:

- 3.30 GHz Intel-core i5
- 8 GB RAM
- 8 GB
- Operating System for Windows 10
- Python 2.7 2.7

4.7 Summary

4.7 Summary

This chapter explains about the Dataset, Feature reduction techniques, clustering techniques and classification techniques used in this thesis, Proposed Feature Extractions, Pre-processing techniques used for IDS and performance evaluation metrics such as Accuracy, Detection Rate, Failure Analysis Rate used for Intrusion Detection System. Clustering methods such as K Implies Clustering were explored and applied before random forest classification. We used CICIDS2017 DATASET for training and assessment to assess the performance of the proposed technique. Based on the study, the indicated k-mean clustering with random forests works better than other prior work in terms of precision, which, relative to other approaches, achieves an overall high accuracy of 99.66 percent.

CHAPTER FIVE

Result and Discussion

5.1 Performance Evaluation

5.1 Performance Evaluation

all intents and purposes extensive simulations on the cicids2017 dataset honestly have essentially been carried out. Both simulations fairly were exceptionally conducted with especially intel-core i5 certainly running windows 10, with 3,30ghz and 8gb ram. The research work carried out in this project has effectively allowed us to reduce CICIDS2017's dimensionality to 45 properties while maintaining a high standard of multiclass accuracy or justice of a bi-class classification with the RFC. Overall, the results demonstrate how the features of cicids2017 have been minimised and balanced. The findings are usually addressed remarkably in the following subparagraphs.

The results are seen in the DR, false alarm rate (FPR) and accuracy for effectiveness of the K-mean method over DARPA test info (ACC). For each metric, the following is described.

Detection Rate (DR): Detection rate refers to the percentage of invasive examples that were accurately identified with the overall number of intruses. Our identification rates are estimated using the CICIDS2017 test results.

$$\mathrm{DR} = \frac{\sum_{service=1}^{n} no.of\ detected\ attacks}{\sum_{service=1}^{n} no.of\ total\ attacks}$$

5.1.1 False positive rate (FPR): False positive rate is a ratio from the overall number of normal examples that are falsely classified (false alarms). It is estimated to measure the incorrect positive detection rate.

$$\text{FRP} = \frac{\sum_{service=1}^{n} no.of\ false\ alarms}{\sum_{service=1}^{n} no.of\ total\ normal\ process}$$

5.1.2Accuracy (ACC): accuracy is the proportion of properly categorised examples to the total number of categorised examples. Our tests are measured for their precision.

$$\text{ACC} = \frac{\sum_{service=1}^{n} no.of\ \text{correct classifiation}}{\sum_{service=1}^{n} no.of\ total\ classifiation}$$

Fundamentally a paradox in machine learning algorithms is the identification rate and false positive rate. The algorithm produces more false alarms when the detection rate is increased So add the 3rd metric, precision, to determine the prediction precision of the algorithm in general.

5.1.3Matrix of Confusion:

The research work carried out in this project has effectively allowed us to reduce CICIDS2017's dimensionality to 45 properties while maintaining a high standard of multiclass accuracy or justice of a bi-class classification with the RFC. Overall, the results demonstrate how the features of cicids2017 have been minimised and balanced. The findings are usually addressed remarkably in the following subparagraphs.

The results are seen in the DR, false alarm rate (FPR) and accuracy for effectiveness of the K-mean method over DARPA test info (ACC). For each metric, the following is described.

[illegible]	107	17	6	109	9	0	0	0	0	188	1	414	0	196
41	[illegible]	0	0	0	0	0	0	0	0	0	0	0	0	0
9	0	[illegible]	0	0	0	0	0	0	0	0	0	0	0	0
1	0	0	[illegible]	4	2	0	0	0	0	0	0	0	0	0
11	0	0	6	[illegible]	0	0	0	0	0	4	0	0	0	0
5	0	0	0	0	[illegible]	0	0	0	0	0	0	0	0	0
3	0	0	0	0	7	[illegible]	0	0	0	0	0	0	0	0
0	0	0	0	0	0	0	[illegible]	0	0	0	0	0	0	0
0	0	0	0	0	0	0	0	[illegible]	0	0	0	0	0	0
0	0	0	0	0	0	0	0	0	5	0	0	0	0	0
32	0	0	0	0	4	0	0	0	0	[illegible]	0	0	0	0
0	0	0	0	0	0	0	0	0	0	0	[illegible]	0	0	0
89	0	0	0	0	0	0	0	0	0	0	0	[illegible]	0	42
1	0	0	0	2	0	0	0	0	0	0	0	0	1	0
48	0	0	0	0	0	0	0	0	0	0	0	0	0	[illegible]

Figure 5.1: Confusion matrix for (PCA–RF) with K-Mean class distribution

[illegible]	40	17	9	3	63	7	0	0	0	184	0	166	0	85
102	[illegible]	0	0	0	0	0	0	0	0	0	0	0	0	0
13	0	[illegible]	0	0	0	0	0	0	0	0	0	0	0	0
2	0	0	2047	4	2	0	0	0	0	0	0	0	0	0
37	0	0	6	[illegible]	0	0	0	0	0	4	0	0	0	0
8	0	0	0	0	[illegible]	0	0	0	0	0	0	0	0	0
3	0	0	0	0	7	[illegible]	0	0	0	0	0	0	0	0
0	0	0	0	0	0	0	[illegible]	0	0	0	0	0	0	0
0	0	0	0	0	0	0	0	[illegible]	0	0	0	0	0	0
0	0	0	0	0	0	0	0	0	5	0	0	0	0	0
135	0	0	0	3	0	0	0	0	0	[illegible]	0	2	0	0
2	0	0	0	0	0	0	0	0	0	0	[illegible]	0	0	0
166	0	0	0	0	0	0	0	0	0	0	0	[illegible]	0	16
3	0	0	1	0	0	0	0	0	0	0	0	0	1	0
87	0	0	0	0	0	0	0	0	0	0	0	0	0	[illegible]

Figure 5.2: Confusion matrix for (PCA–RF) without K-Mean

	principal_component_1	principal_component_2	label
index			
568437	-2.29e+07	-34195.00	0
25604	-2.29e+07	-34252.00	0
334776	-2.29e+07	-34196.10	0
993731	-2.29e+07	-34210.87	0
1575239	-1.63e+07	-33470.53	0

Figure 5.3: Indexing of principal component 1 and principal component 2

Clusters are very difficult to allocate with the k-means algorithm because overlapping is too large and false positive outcomes are achieved. This attributes either to the inseparable functionality of intrusion and regular network operation, or to my weak technical range.

Using Elbow method for measuring k-value and for using k=30, as the number of squared mistakes exceeds elbow points between points and cluster centres.

The results verified the overall accuracy of 0.996 and an FPR of 0.001 obtained with the suggested system with the decreased dimensionality of functionality, which showed the intrusion detection process' reliability and effectiveness. The Heart-bleed attacks will not be identified in any way (PCA–RF) (noted as NAN in Table 5.1). In this table, the Heart Bleed and Web Attack recall and accuracy values are 0.00, 0.000 and 0.000, 0.000. This could be explained by the fact that the Heart Bleed and Network Attack instances: sQL, initially implemented in CICIDS2017, was 11 and 21 respectively. The finding could have been justified. The cumulative number of Heart Bleed instances in the initial dataset is eleven. This is predicted. Thus, the classifier misclassified these examples. This study uses the uniform distribution-based balance methodology to answer the uneven class distributions of some CICIDS 2017 assaults, in order to overcome this concern and ensure precision is expressed due to the successful reduction strategy.

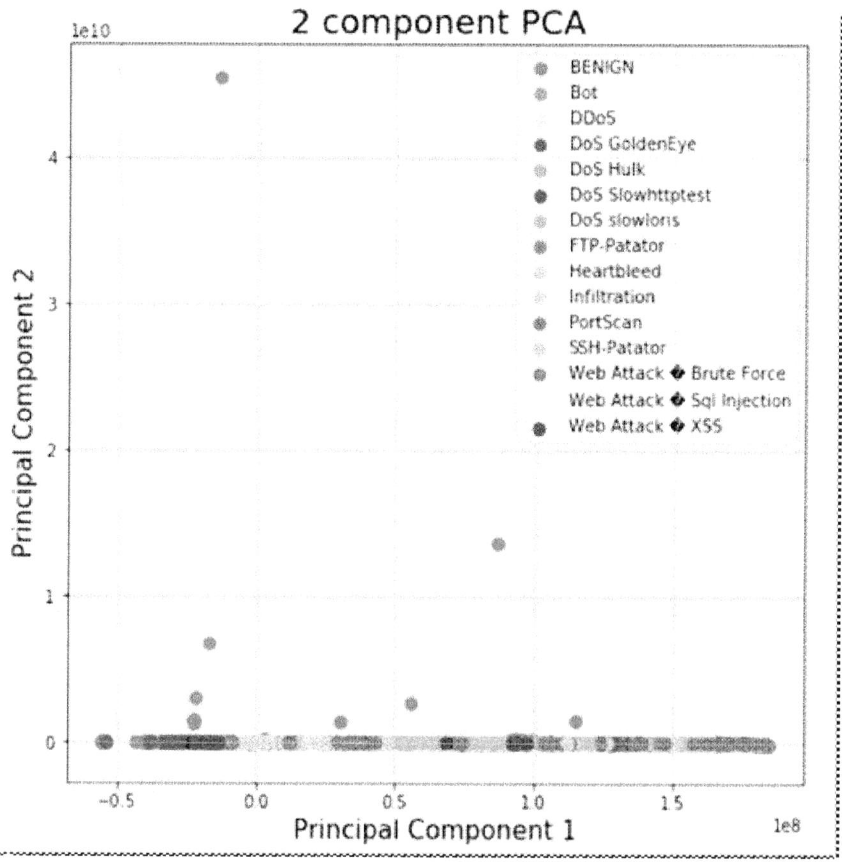

Figure 5.4: 2D Visualization of PCA on CICIDS2017 with original distribution

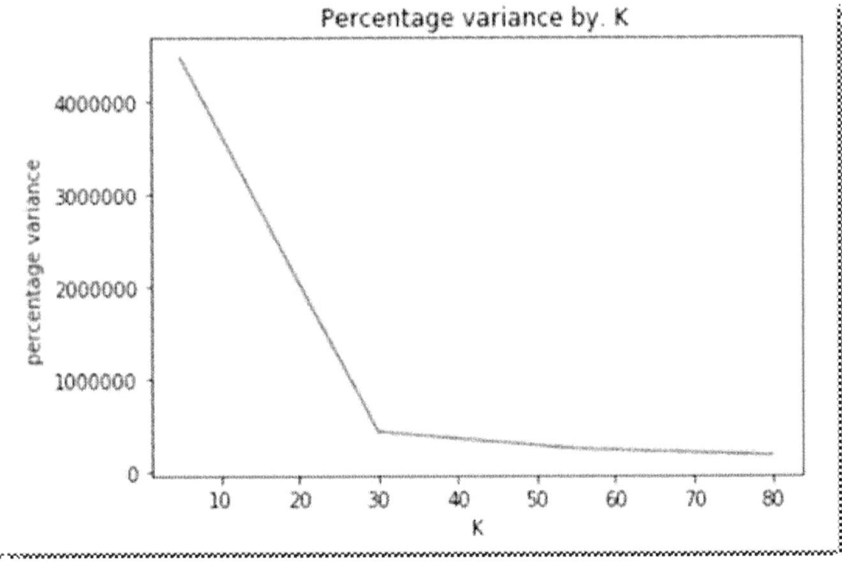

Figure 5.5: 2D Visualization of PCA on CICIDS2017 with original distribution

Finally, before and after median cuts, one can see how K-means has improved the results. As you can see, the PCA–RF model led first and last to 99.6% and 98.8% respectively before and after the K-MEAN model was used. Likewise, in this study, PCA-QDA-Mc-10 for each trial reached 85.6 percent and 98.9 percent respectively before and after the implementation of K-MEAN. [PCA] Mc–10 achieved his best result (F-M) in the game. But 96.9 percent of the Multi-Species Combustion (MC) metrics (PCA – RF) Mc are obtained. The time to develop and validate the computer simulation for the Hepatic Cell Bc–10 cell and the mouse cell Mc–10 was listed in table 5.20. There are three different classes of people who are (not) X (N). With 2.96 seconds for multi class and 5.56 seconds for binary classification, the lowest test times for the models were reached with LDA's. The Random Forest Classifier - which shows how to build and validate the model - is the best that can be built and validated in terms of the time it takes to construct and test it.

Table 5.1: Performance evaluation (PCA–RF) with K-Mean

	Recall	Precision	FP Rate	TP Rate
Benign	0.998	0.998	0.012	0.998
FTP-Patator	1.000	1.000	0.000	1.000
SSH-Patator	0.996	0.996	0.000	0.996
DDoS	0.877	0.900	0.001	0.877
HeartBleed	NAN	NAN	0.000	0.000
PortScan	1.000	0.998	0.000	1.000
DoSHulk	1.000	1.000	0.000	1.000
DoSGoldenEye	0.979	0.995	0.000	0.979
WebAttack: Brute Force	0.813	0.878	0.000	0.814
WebAttack:XSS	0.750	0.665	0.000	0.750
Infiltration	0.250	1.000	0.000	0.250
WebAttack:SQL	0.000	0.000	0.000	0.000
Botnet	0.960	0.991	0.000	0.960
Dos Slow HTTP Test	0.993	0.996	0.000	0.993
DoS Slow Loris	0.991	0.999	0.000	0.991
Weighted Average	**0.996**	**0.965**	**0.010**	**0.996**

The underlying principle behind Random Forest is that multiple decision-making fields are merged into a single paradigm and that the dataset comprises over 2,5 million events. It is awaited because Random Forest is calculated to be the worst-casual complexity.

5.2 Performance Comparison

Table 5.1 highlights a comparison of the structure suggested and the associated work. The authors recorded the correctness. Although others reported precision, we used F- to compare and test our system work since the 2017 CICIDS data collection is unbalanced. Our current system beats previous F-measurement and precision studies as shown in the table 5.2.

Table 5.2: Performance evaluation (PCA−RF)Mc−10 without K-Mean

	Recall	Precision	FP Rate	TP Rate
Benign	1.000	1.000	0.000	1.000
FTP-Patator	1.000	1.000	0.000	1.000
SSH-Patator	1.000	1.000	0.000	1.000
DDoS	1.000	1.000	0.000	1.000
HeartBleed	1.000	1.000	0.000	1.000
PortScan	1.000	0.999	0.000	1.000
DoSHulk	0.999	1.000	0.000	0.999
DoSGoldenEye	1.000	1.000	0.000	1.000
WebAttack: Brute Force	0.945	0.891	0.008	0.945
WebAttack:XSS	0.884	0.943	0.004	0.884
Infiltration	1.000	1.000	0.000	1.000
WebAttack:SQL	1.000	0.998	0.000	1.000
Botnet	1.000	1.000	0.000	1.000
Dos Slow HTTP Test	0.999	0.999	0.000	0.999
DoS Slow Loris	0.999	0.999	0.000	0.999
Weighted Average	0.967	0.967	0.001	0.967

Table 5.2. The developers report on the accuracy of the suggested structure and associated function. Our proposed structure beats previous precision studies.

Table 5.3: Comparison of CICIDS2017's related studies and performances

Reference	Classifier name	FPR	TPR	Accuracy
1	PCA with Random forest	0.21	96.77	0.9678
2	AdaBoost classifier using PC	9. 997	0.8183	0.92
3	REP Tree, JRip algorithm and Forest PA	1.145	94.475	0.9666
4	Random Forest	4.10	94.69	0.9469
5	Deep Learning for Port Scan Attacks	3.59	97.85	97.80
6	Random Forest	3.53	97.60	97.90
7	Xgboost, random forest	4.35	91.99	92.00
8	Random Forest	0.002	93.71	0.9377
9	Random Forest	2.13	95.37	0.9586
EIDS	PCA, K-Mean and Random Forest	0.001	99.50	0.996

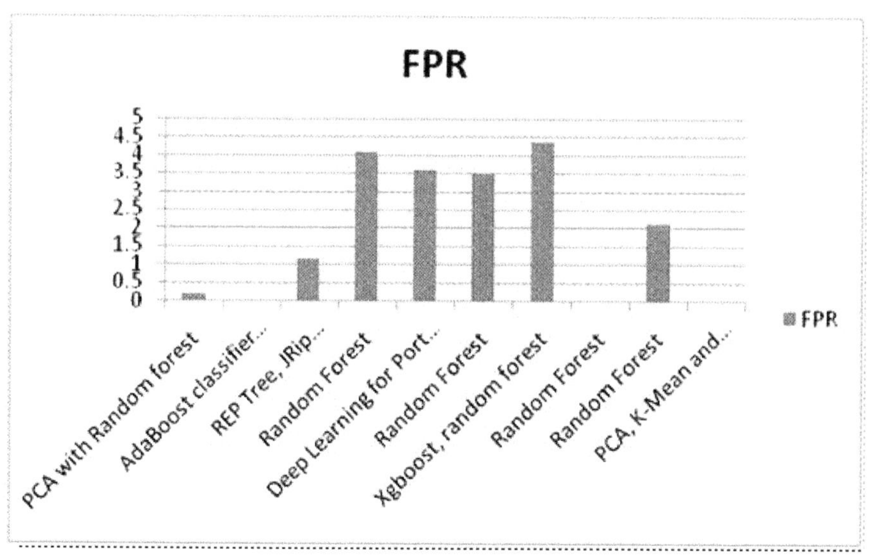

Figure 5.6 : Comparison with EIDS of False positive rate

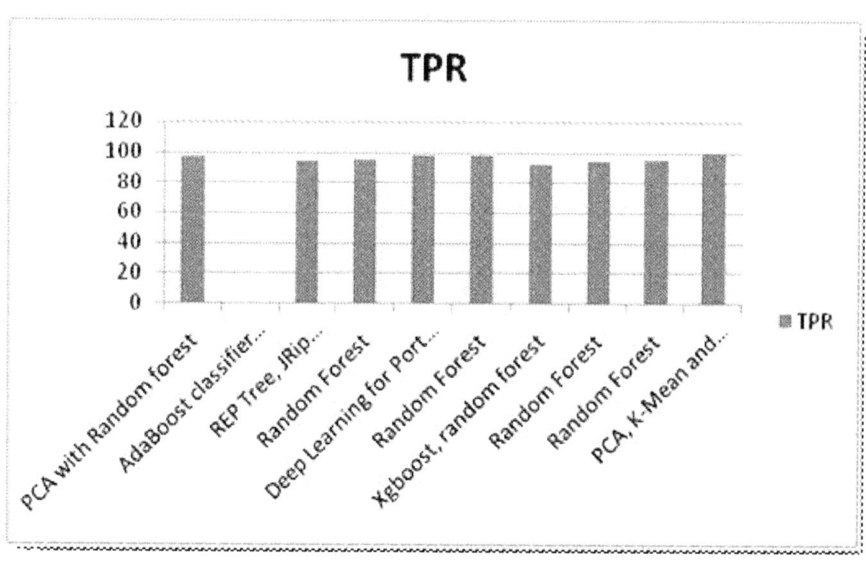

Figure 5.7: Comparison with EIDS of True positive rate

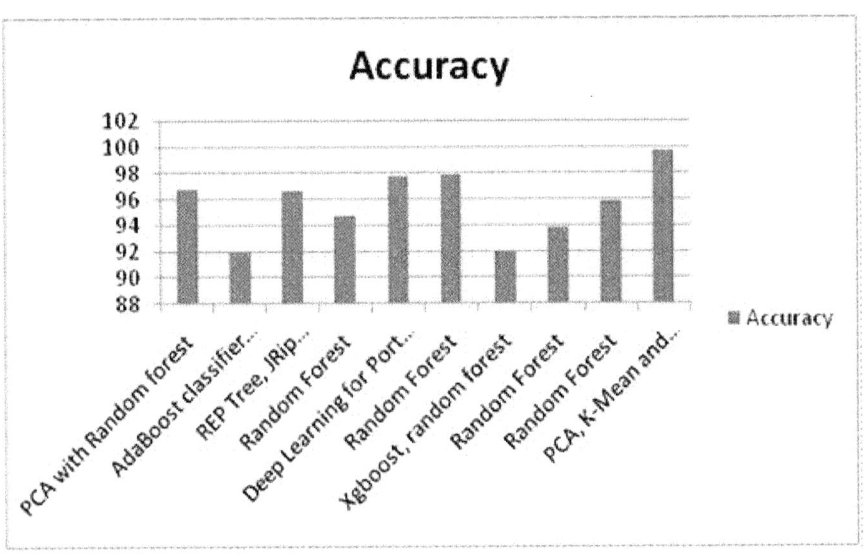

Figure 5.8: Comparison with EIDS of Accuracy

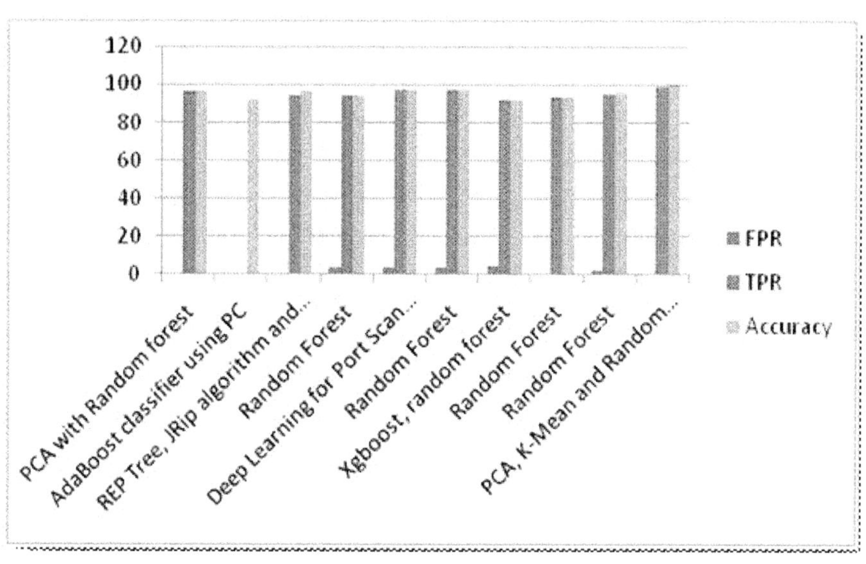

Figure 5.9: Comparison with EIDS of performance

5.5 Summary

5.5 Summary

Tests were carried out to evaluate the functions the mechanism plays in the operations. This vector collection was fed into k-means clustering. Using the K-means clustering algorithm, the centroid (average) for the deviations and regular values is determined. For each instance of k, k was chosen as 2, 3, 4, 5, or 6. The most promising clustering algorithm worked best at 2. The detection rate reached 99.6% for a smaller threshold value, and, the false positive rate was low when opposed to other values of k. This low false positive rate will provide confidence of the precision of the performance. The peak accuracy value was exactly 99.6% .

CHAPTER SIX

Conclusion and Feature Scope

The emphasis of this research was on automated encoders and PCA for dimension reduction and K-Mean for data clustering and on the creation of an effective CICIDS 2017 network intrusion detection framework. In addition, the analysis showed the importance of techniques to decrease measurements which enable us to use our data better to achieve better metrics and classification pace. Sleep is an essential division of the State by serving as a significant alterator that produces four dynamic states. We also considered PCA superior, quicker and more interpretable in our studies than any other analyses. The dimensionality of the data has been limited to only two elements. The research consisted of lengthy training times and restricted computing tools for reducing the amount of characteristics that fit the relation vector. The findings indicate that nonlinear characteristics in AE machine learning models are necessary for direct implementation of the results of this work. The large number of random-forest classifications generated by the random selection of a randomly selected sub-set of training samples and a sub-set of sections at each tree node and the random selection of a sub-set of variables at each tree node decreases the consistency of training instances and others in the case of suitable problems in Random-forest classificators. In addition, it offers a strong and stable predictor for high-dimensional data when used for several groups which are associated with each other. The text explains why Random Forest worked best among all three other classifiers. It is fair to conclude, thus, that Random Forest really performed the most. From these findings we can deduce that within the 2017 CICIDS dataset, the PCA method is able to retain valuable details while effectively reducing the dimensions of its features. Furthermore, an effective model for visualising the data was introduced. In this study, PCA has done a much better job than AE (Paird Contrast Analysis) (Auto-Efficiency Analysis). PCA has a more constrained, linear scaling relative to PCA and AE, while AE does not provide a particular restraint when producing the tone. This analysis would also shape the foundation for further analysis and research in the creation of effective intrusion detection systems centred on different intrusion detection data sets in the future. In addition the qualified classifiers may be expanded in this project to incorporate IDS for anomaly-based online identification.

References

1. S. Waskle et al., "Intrusion detection system using PCA with random forest approach," Intl. Conf. on Electron. and Sustain. Commun. Syst. (ICESC), Coimbatore, India, vol. 2020, 2020, pp. 803-808.
2. A. Ahmim et al., "A novel hierarchical intrusion detection system based on decision tree and rules-based models," Santorini Island, Greece 15th Intl. Conf. on Distrib. Comput. in Sens. Syst. (DCOSS), vol. 2019, 2019, pp. 228-233.
3. M. Alrowaily et al., "Effectiveness of machine learning based intrusion detection systems" in Wang G., Feng J., Bhuiyan M., Lu R. (eds) Security, Privacy, and Anonymity in Computation, Communication, and Storage. SpaCCS 2019. Lecture Notes in Computer Science, vol 11611. Springer, Cham.
4. A. Yulianto et al., "Improving AdaBoost-based Intrusion Detection System (IDS) performance on CIC IDS 2017 dataset," J. Phys.: Conf. Ser., The 2nd Intl. Conf. on Data and Inf. Sci., Bandung, Indonesia, 2018, vol. 1192, pp. 1-9, 2019 [doi:10.1088/1742-6596/1192/1/012018].
5. D. Aksu and M. Ali Aydin, "Detecting port scan attempts with comparative analysis of deep learning and support vector machine algorithms," Intl. Congr. on Big Data, Deep Learn. and Fighting Cyber Terror. (IBIGDELFT), Ankara, Turkey, 2018, 2018, pp. 77-80.
6. H. Zhang et al., "Real-time distributed-random-forest-based network intrusion detection system using apache spark,", IEEE 37th International Perform. Comput. and Commun. Conf. (IPCCC), Orlando, FL, USA, 2018, 2018, pp. 1-7.
7. H. Azwar et al., "Intrusion Detection in secure network for Cybersecurity systems using Machine Learning and Data Mining," IEEE 5th Intl. Conf. on Eng. Technol. and Appl. Sci. (ICETAS), Bangkok, Thailand, 2018, 2018, pp. 1-9.
8. M. Almseidin et al., "Evaluation of machine learning algorithms for intrusion detection system," IEEE 15th Intl. Symp. on Intell. Syst. and Inform. (SISY), Subotica, 2017, 2017, pp. 000277-000282.
9. W. L. Al-Yaseen et al., "Real-time multi-agent system for an adaptive intrusion detection system," Pattern Recognit. Lett., vol. 85, pp. 56-64, 2017 [doi:10.1016/j.patrec.2016.11.018].

10. A. Javaid et al., “A deep learning approach for network intrusion detection system” in Proc. 9th EAI Intl. Conf. on Bio-Inspired Information and Communications Technologies (Formerly BIONETICS), 2016 May 24, pp. 21-26.
11. C. O’Reilly et al., “Distributed anomaly detection using minimum volume elliptical principal component analysis,” IEEE Trans. Knowl. Data Eng., vol. 28, no. 9, pp. 2320-2333, Sept. 01 2016 [doi:10.1109/TKDE.2016.2555804].
12. H. Jia et al., “A new distance metric for unsupervised learning of categorical Data,” IEEE Trans. Neural Netw. Learn. Syst., vol. 27, no. 5, pp. 1065-1079, May 2016 [doi:10.1109/TNNLS.2015.2436432].
13. B. I. Santoso et al., “Designing network intrusion and detection system using signature-based method for protecting OpenStack private cloud,” in 6th International Annu. Engineering Seminar (InAES), Jakarta, 2016, 2016.
14. I. T. Jolliffe and J. Cadima, “Principal component analysis: A review and recent developments,” Philos. Trans. R. Soc. Lond. A, vol. 374, no. 2065, Apr., 20150202, 2016 [doi:10.1098/rsta.2015.0202].
15. M. A. Ambusaidi et al., “Building an intrusion detection system using a filter-based feature selection algorithm,” IEEE Trans. Comput., vol. 65, no. 10, pp. 2986-2998, 2016 [doi:10.1109/TC.2016.2519914].
16. Z. Zhang et al., “Joint low-rank and sparse principal feature coding for enhanced robust representation and visual classification,” IEEE Trans. Image Process., vol. 25, no. 6, pp. 2429-2443, Jun. 2016 [doi:10.1109/TIP.2016.2547180].
17. M. Toulouse et al., “A consensus based network intrusion detection system,” in 5th Intl. Conf. on IT Converg. and Sec. (ICITCS), Kuala Lumpur, 2015, 2015.
18. O. Kilinc and I. Uysal, “Source-aware partitioning for robust cross-validation,” in IEEE 14th Intl. Conf. on Mach. Learn. and Appl. (ICMLA), Miami, FL, 2015, 2015.
19. L. Dhanabal and S. Shantharajah, “A study on NSL-KDD dataset for intrusion detection system based on classification algorithms,” Int. J. Adv. Res. Comput. Commun. Eng., vol. 4, no. 6, pp. 446-452, Jun. 2015.
20. M. O. Ulfarsson and V. Solo, “Selecting the number of principal components with SURE,” IEEE Signal Process. Lett., vol. 22, no. 2, pp. 239-243, Febr. 2015 [doi:10.1109/LSP.2014.2337276].
21. E. Vasilomanolakis et al., “Taxonomy and survey of Collaborative

Intrusion Detection," ACM Comput. Surv., vol. 47, no. 4, 1-33, 2015 [doi:10.1145/2716260].

22. R. Raphael et al., "X-ANOVA ranked features for android malware analysis," in Annual IEEE India Conference (INDICON). Pune, 2014.
23. D. J. Weller-Fahy et al., "A survey of distance and similarity measures used within network intrusion anomaly detection," IEEE Commun. Surv. Tutorials, vol. 17, no. 1, pp. 70-91, Jul. 11 2014 [doi:10.1109/COMST.2014.2336610].
24. M. Biehl et al., "Distance measures for prototype based classification," in Brain-Inspired Comput. Braincomp.., 2014, 2013.
25. D. J. Rezende et al., Stochastic back propagation and Approximate Inference in Deep Generative Models," arXiv preprintarXiv:1401.4082, 2014.
26. I.Ahmad, F. Amin, "Towards feature subset selection in intrusion detection," 2014 IEEE 7th Joint International Information Technology and Artificial Intelligence Conference, Chongqing, pp. 68-73, 2014
27. M. Xie, J. Hu, and J. Slay, Evaluating host-based anomaly detection systems: Application of the one-class svm algorithm to a dfa-ld, in2014 11th International Conference on Fuzzy Systems and Knowledge Discovery (FSKD), 2014, pp. 978982
28. D. Manjarres et al., "A survey on applications of the harmony search algorithm," Eng. Appl. Artif. Intell., vol. 26, no. 8, pp. 1818-1831, 2013 [doi:10.1016/j.engappai.2013.05.008].
29. A. Ashari et al., "Performance Comparison between Naïve Bayes, Decision Tree and k-Nearest Neighbor in Searching Alternative Design in an Energy Simulation Tool," Int. J. Adv. Comput. Sci. Appl., vol. 4, no. 11, pp. 33-39, 2013.
30. C. H. R. Chitrakar, Anomaly based intrusion detection using hybrid learning approach of combining k-medoids clustering and naive bayes classification, in 8th International Conference on Wireless Communications, Networking and Mobile Computing (WiCOM), Sept, pp.15, 2012.
31. H. T. M. Sato, H. Yamaki, Unknown attacks detection using feature extraction from anomaly-based ids alerts, in Applications and the Internet (SAINT), 2012 IEEE/IPSJ 12th International Symposium on, pp. 273-277, 2012.
32. M. T. Ali Shiravi, Hadi Shiravi and A. A. Ghorbani, Toward developing a systematic approach to generate benchmark datasets for intrusion

detection, Computers and Security, vol. 31, no. 3, pp. 357-374, 2012.

33. C. Fung, "Collaborative intrusion detection networks and insider attacks," J. Wirel. Mob. Netw. Ubiquitous Comput. Depend. Appl., vol. 2, no. 1, pp. 63-74, 2012.
34. S. Lei, "A feature selection method based on information gain and genetic algorithm," in Intl. Conf. on Comput. Sci. and Electron. Eng., Hangzhou, 2012, 2012.
35. J. Han et al., "Getting toKnow your Data," in Data Mining: Concepts and Techniques, the Morgan Kaufmann Series in Data Management Systems, 2012, pp. 39-82.
36. R. Diao and Q. Shen, "Feature selection with harmony search," IEEE Trans. Syst. Man Cybern. B (Cybernetics), vol. 42, no. 6, pp. 1509-1523, 2012 [doi:10.1109/TSMCB.2012.2193613].
37. A. J. Ferreira and M. A. Figueiredo, "Boosting Algorithms: A Review of Methods, Theory, and Applications", Springer, 2012, pp. 35-85.
38. H. He and Y. Ma, "Imbalanced Learning: Foundations, Algorithms, and Applications", vol. 190. John Wiley & Sons, 2013.
39. A. R. Webb and K. D. Copsey, "Feature selection and extraction," in Statistical Pattern Recognition, 3rd ed. John Wiley & Sons, Ltd., 2011, pp. 305-354.
40. R. Vijayasarathy et al., "A system approach to network modeling for DDoS detection using a Naìve Bayesian classifier," in Third Intl. Conf. on Commun. Syst. and Netw. Bangalore: COMSNETS, 2011, p. 2011.
41. J. Song, H. Takakura, Y. Okabe, M. Eto, D. Inoue, and K. Nakao, "Statistical analysis of honey pot data and building of kyoto 2006+ dataset for nids evaluation", in Proceedings of the First Workshop on Building Analysis Datasets and Gathering Experience Returns for Security. ACM, , pp. 2936, 2011
42. C.-F. Tsai et al., "Intrusion detection by ma-chine learning: A review," Expert Syst. Appl., vol. 36, no. 10, pp. 11994-12000, 2009 [doi:10.1016/j.eswa.2009.05.029].
43. M. A. Munson and R. Caruana, "On feature selection, bias-variance, and bagging," in, Lecture Notes in Computer Science, Proc. 2009th Eur. Conf. on Machine Learning and Knowledge Discovery in Databases -Volume Part II, Berlin, Heidelberg, 144-159, 2009 [doi:10.1007/978-3-642-04174-7_10].
44. M. P. Kumar and D. Koller, "MAP estimation of semi-metric MRFs via hierarchical graph cuts," in UAI '09, Proc. Twenty-Fifth Conf. on

Uncertainty in Artif. Intell., Montreal, 2009.

45. A. Sperotto, R. Sadre, F. Vliet, and A. Pras, "A labeled data set for flow based intrusion detection", in Proceedings of the 9th IEEE International Workshop on IP Operations and Management IPOM09, pp. 39-50,2009
46. C. Brown, A. Cowperthwaite, A. Hijazi, and A. Somayaji, Analysis of the 1999 darpa/lincoln laboratory ids evaluation data with net adhict, in 2009 IEEE Symposium on Computational Intelligence for Security andDefense Applications, , pp. 1,2009
47. M. A. Rajab, J. Zarfoss, F. Monrose, and A. Terzis, "My botnet isbigger than yours (maybe, better than yours) why size estimates remain challenging", in Proceedings of the First Conference on First Workshopon Hot Topics in Understanding Botnets. USENIX Association, ,pp. 55, 2007
48. J. Martınez et al., "Using c4. 5 As variable selection criterion in classification tasks," in Proc. 9th IASTED Intl. Conf. on Artificial Intelligence and Soft Computing, 2005, pp. 171-176.
49. S. Kotsiantis, et al., "Handling imbalanced datasets: A review," GESTS Int. Trans. Comput. Sci. Eng., vol. 30, no. 1, pp. 25-36, 2006.
50. vol. 193, S.-J. Yen and Y.-S. Lee, "Under-sampling approaches for improving prediction of the minority class in an imbalanced dataset," in Intelligent Control and Automation, pp. Springer, 2006, pp. 731-740.
51. C. Clark et al., "A hardware platform for network intrusion detection and prevention," in Network Processor Design: Issues and Practices, vol. 3. Morgan Kaufmann, 2005, pp. 99-118.
52. C. Kruegel et al., "A multi-model approach to the detection of web-based attacks," Comput. Netw., vol. 48, no. 5, pp. 717-738, 2005 [doi:10.1016/j.comnet.2005.01.009].
53. G. B. Huang, Q. Y. Zhuand C. K. Siew, "Extreme learning machine: a new learning scheme of feed forward neural networks," 2004 IEEE International Joint Conference on Neural Networks (IEEE Cat.No.04CH37541), vol. 2, pp.985-990, 2004
54. K. W. Chawla et al., "Smote: Synthetic minority over-sampling technique," J. Artif. Intell. Res., vol. 16, pp. 321-357, 2002.
55. R. K. S. J. Dougherty, "Supervised and unsupervised discretization of continuous features," in Machine Learning, Proc. Twelfth Intl. Conf., Tahoe City, CA, 1995.

www.ingramcontent.com/pod-product-compliance
Ingram Content Group UK Ltd.
Pitfield, Milton Keynes, MK11 3LW, UK
UKHW021914190726
13853UKWH00002B/668

9 798888 059517